How to
Expand Your
S.I.Q.
(Social
Intelligence Quotient)

How to Expand Your S.I.Q.
(Social Intelligence Quotient)

By Dane Archer, Ph.D.

Photographs by Arlene Burney and Rick Bender

M. Evans and Company, Inc. New York

Library of Congress Cataloging in Publication Data

Archer, Dane.
  How to expand your S.I.Q. (social intelligence
quotient)

  Bibliography: p.
  1. Social perception. 2. Nonverbal communica-
tion.
I. Title.
HM132.A67   301.11   79-19568
ISBN 0-87131-286-7
ISBN 0-87131-296-4 pbk.

M. Evans and Company, Inc.
216 East 49 Street
New York, New York 10017

Design by Ginger Giles

Manufactured in the United States of America

9 8 7 6 5 4 3 2 1

CONTENTS

for Mary Frances, of course

How to
Expand Your
S.I.Q.
(Social
Intelligence Quotient)

PREFACE

Social intelligence is the ability to understand people—their relationships, their feelings, their concerns, and their individuality. This book provides each of us with a chance to increase our social intelligence by learning about the nonverbal clues that make it possible.

The book is built around a series of photographs. Each photograph shows one person or several people together. The photographs were taken in a variety of locations—on the street, in restaurants and stores, and outdoors. Each picture is paired with a specific social intelligence question. Each question has a correct answer, and clues to the answer are found in the photograph.

These social intelligence pictures and questions were shown to a total of twenty-four hundred "judges"—people who looked at the photographs and tried to guess the answers to the social intelligence questions. The accuracy of our judges on each question is reported so that the reader can tell how "easy" or "difficult" each photograph is. In addition, the comments our judges made about the pictures are summarized so that readers can expand their own social intelligence by sharing in the perceptions and insights of this large group of judges.

A project of this scale would have been impossible without the help of some friends and many strangers. This help starts with the photographs themselves. Arlene Burney took most of the original pictures in this book. Arlene was a student in my course on nonverbal communication at the University of California, Santa Cruz, and I soon realized that she was the perfect person to shoot the photographs for this book. The best evidence of her success is the spontaneous and splendidly candid quality of her pictures.

Arlene worked entirely in the "field"; none of these photographs was taken in a studio. She showed great courage in her willingness to approach complete strangers with what must have seemed like strange requests. Fortunately, most people responded positively. Some people were unexpectedly enthusiastic, and Arlene is probably the only person to have been hugged in the line of duty. Arlene somehow manages to capture people on film without making them freeze or change in any way. For this reason, I think her pictures are an unusually accurate window on people in actual situations.

Many people helped in the testing of our twenty-four hundred judges. Debra D. Kimes and Michael Barrios, two former students and current friends, recruited the lion's share of this large sample of judges. These two people also summarized some of the comments our judges made about individual photographs. Two other former students and current friends, Rick Bender and Judy Schwartz, also recruited large numbers of judges. Rick Bender took some of the original photographs in this book. Four other people—John W. Hartmire, Kevin Renner, Karen Tanji, and Anne Morykwas—tested some of our judges.

I would also like to express my appreciation to Robert Rosenthal and Robin Akert, because even though they were not involved in this book, they have been extremely valuable colleagues in my earlier research on nonverbal communication. In addition, I have discussed aspects of this book with my friend and colleague John I. Kitsuse, and his comments have been extremely helpful. Herbert Katz and Linda Cabasin contributed encouragement and a fine editorial sense.

Some of the most important people in the making of this book were the many friends and strangers who agreed to be photographed. I think this was an act of considerable courage. Even when we pose for a casual photograph, most of us are concerned about the way we look. When people posed for these photographs, they knew they would be seen by many people—our twenty-four hundred judges and the readers of this book. They also knew that the people who saw the photographs would be trying to answer questions—sometimes very personal questions—about the people in the pictures. I am grateful for the courage of the people who were willing to be photographed. Without them, this kind of book about social intelligence would have been impossible.

This book also benefited from the help of more than two thousand perfect strangers, our judges. These twenty-four hundred people were kind enough to spend some time looking at photographs and trying to answer questions about the people in them. Fortunately, most of our judges seemed to enjoy this assignment. Even though these judges are anonymous, their answers and comments have enriched every part of this book.

Finally, this project was greatly assisted by Mary Frances Archer. Some of her contributions were to the more onerous phases of the project. She helped duplicate more than seventy-two hundred pages of social intelligence questions, and she did some of the coding to prepare answer sheets for computer analysis. Mary Fran also read most of the thirty thousand individual comments our judges made in response to the social intelligence questions. She read through this mountain of data with a sensitive eye for rare and revealing clues.

But more than all these things, Mary Fran has contributed encouragement and intellectual partnership to this project. We have spent uncounted hours discussing social intelligence, and I have always found her observations of people to be breathtakingly accurate. I am indebted for the way she has shared this gift, and many others, with me over the years. Zachary Keller and Nathaniel Dylan Archer are two of these gifts. My sons also deserve to be mentioned, since, in a very different way, they give me a chance to see the world again as if for the first time.

1 SOCIAL INTELLIGENCE

Intelligence is a complex psychological concept. The layman may think of intelligence as the general mental ability involved in reasoning and learning. I.Q. tests reveal the dominant way in which we have thought about intelligence; in fact, a witticism popular among psychologists is that "intelligence is whatever the I.Q. tests test." Most I.Q. tests include questions about the definitions of words, analogies, and the meaning of phrases. This is an extraordinary verbal bias. These tests measure how well a person can comprehend words. Even when drawings are included in I.Q. tests, these drawings tend to be of mathematical shapes or abstract figures. People are never shown. The ability measured by I.Q. tests is, therefore, verbal intelligence.

Psychologists and sociologists have long suspected that there is another, quite different kind of intelligence. This second kind of intelligence is thought to consist of the ability to form accurate interpretations about people—their experiences, their individual characteristics, their relationships, their concerns, and their emotions. Until recently, there has been almost no research in this area, perhaps because of a general verbal bias in Western society.

This very different type of ability is called social intelligence, and it might be roughly defined as "the ability to form accurate interpretations about people." There is already some evidence that this people-oriented ability is different from verbal intelligence. In fact, the two abilities appear to be largely unrelated. A person can be strong in both verbal intelligence and social intelligence, or be strong in one but not the other, or even be weak in both.

In a sense, folk theories about intelligence have made this distinction for a long time. We all have heard someone described as very bright but not good at understanding people. This is one way of describing a person strong in verbal intelligence but weak in social intelligence. Clearly, these folk theories reflect the belief that just because a person is verbally intelligent, he or she is not necessarily a good judge of people. In finding that these two abilities are different, recent research merely provides scientific support for a long-held public belief.

Even though we may differ in our ability, most of us use our social intelligence every day. It is probably no exaggeration to suggest that society as we know it would be impossible without social intelligence, although this seems to be an ability we use without awareness. We generally use our social intelligence automatically or unconsciously. The largely unconscious nature of social intelligence has undoubtedly contributed to the relative neglect of this topic in social science research.

General Social Intelligence

Each one of us possesses two types of social intelligence. The first type is what I call *general social intelligence.* This refers to knowledge and skills that are shared by most or all members of a society or culture. Without our general social intelligence, society would be impossible.

We use our general social intelligence every day. Each of us has known hundreds or even thousands of people in our lifetime, but somehow we are able to distinguish among their faces. When we see a friend or acquaintance on the street, we can recognize the person. This act of recognition is a miracle of general social intelligence, and yet each of us performs it—unconsciously—many times each day.

Our ability to recognize people is obviously complex, since we can identify the unique features of each of the many people we know. Few of us, however, would be able to explain how we do this. For example, try to describe in words, and in great detail, exactly what a friend looks like. When I try this, my description is never precise enough—it could fit every tenth or twentieth person on the street. We cannot describe in words the visual clues that we "know" and use every day. I think this demonstrates that our general social intelligence is greater than our verbal ability to describe it.

There are hundreds of other examples of general social intelligence. Most of us also recognize our friends when they call on the telephone, before they identify themselves. This indicates that we have a complex ability to distinguish among hundreds of individual voices, just as we distinguish among faces. Again, this miracle of general social intelligence is difficult to explain. For example, I cannot describe what is unique about my friends' voices, but I have no trouble telling them apart on the telephone.

Even when complete strangers call us on the telephone, our general social intelligence comes to our aid. We can almost always recognize whether our caller is a man or a woman. In addition, I think we can guess the caller's age within ten years—this is another impressive example of our general social intelligence. We might be hard pressed to explain how the voices of a thirty-year-old and a forty-year-old differ, but we have little trouble recognizing this difference when we answer the telephone.

There are many other ways in which our general social intelligence informs us about people from their voices alone. Sociologists have shown recently that we can guess how much education people have had from their voices, even when they just recite the alphabet. Voices also may reveal our ethnicity and the region of the country from which we come. Again, even though we might be unable to say what clues we use in making these judgments, it is clear that we can make them fairly accurately.

The most ordinary interactions would be awkward or impossible without these types of unconscious knowledge. When we have a conversation with someone, for example, most of us can tell when the other person wants to talk. But how do we know this, and what are the clues we use? Clearly, we are not given verbal clues. Imagine a friend saying, "I would like to speak now." Most of us can tell when it is time to end a phone call or leave a dinner or party. We can tell when a person is in a hurry and whether he or she has time to talk with us. But the nonverbal clues we use are rarely made explicit, and it would be hard for us to say how we know all these things.

Even our physical movements are guided by our general

social intelligence. When we stop to talk to a friend on the street, we all know precisely how close—within one or two inches—to stand to the person so that he or she will feel comfortable. This area of social intelligence is so precise that when we meet someone important or famous, we unconsciously stand farther from the individual than we would from the average person. This is an area of general social intelligence in which there are national rules. When we meet people from another country, they may stand so close to us that we feel crowded and uneasy. When foreigners stand too close to us, they unwittingly break our national rules regarding speaking distance.

When people are traveling in another country, they inevitably break many national rules. This is why we frequently are able to spot tourists and other foreigners. A few years ago, I was on a bus in Princeton, New Jersey, and was seated in the last row of seats. A couple boarded at a bus stop, and something about the way the man carefully searched through a handful of coins struck me as an important clue. It seems to me that foreigners tend to pay for things very slowly due to their lack of familiarity with an alien currency. In addition, on the basis of their haircuts and clothes, I guessed they were German tourists. As explained later in this book, I think it is terribly important for us to be able to test our social intelligence. For this reason, I wanted to see if my interpretation was accurate. When the bus halted at my stop, I walked toward the front and slowed as I passed the couple. I was gratified to hear the man say to his companion, *"Das ist echt ein schönes Dorf."*

Behaving in a "foreign" manner can sometimes have serious consequences, at least in fiction. For example, the plot of one movie about World War II concerned American agents who had been trained in German language and customs so they would be able to pass undetected in Germany itself. One of the agents, however, committed an unmistakably foreign act while in a German restaurant. After cutting a piece of meat, the agent switched the fork from his left to his right hand. This is expected etiquette for Americans, but Germans never do it. Nazi officers present in the restaurant immediately arrested the man as a foreign agent. Despite his careful training, this fictional American failed to "perform" German nationality in an authentic manner.

There are many other areas of life in which our actions are

guided, even if unconsciously, by our general social intelligence. For example, most of us can walk down a crowded sidewalk without bumping into other people. Clearly, we "decode" the movements and intentions of other pedestrians so we can calculate the best direction or evasive action to take. Since the other pedestrians are also making these calculations, a collision sometimes results. These mistakes can be embarrassing, but they are the exceptions that prove the general rule that we "navigate" rather well most of the time.

Our general social intelligence also makes it possible for us to interpret other people's behavior. For example, all of us can recognize someone who is drunk, and some of us may feel we can recognize a "crazy" person. Some of the clues we use are clear— such as the drunk's stumble or slurred speech—but others are much more subtle. In recognizing a crazy person, is it enough to detect a vacant or unfocused gaze, or do we look for mumbling and other signs? Drunks and crazy people clearly break social rules in a way that leads us to label their behavior in these terms. The important thing about this is that we clearly have an unconscious knowledge of the "normal" way to walk, talk, interact, and look. This is an important part of our general social intelligence. When people break these unconscious rules, we are likely to think of them as strange or deviant in some way.

We also use our general social intelligence to "read" our friends. We can almost always tell when a friend is very happy. This is true even when the friend tries to hide this fact from us—for example, by modestly concealing a recent triumph. We can also use our general social intelligence to alter our interpretation of specific nonverbal clues. A person's tears or crying usually indicate sadness, but none of us would conclude that the sobbing of a newly crowned Miss America indicates sadness or that crying at the end of a sentimental movie indicates anything but pleasure. Our general social intelligence is so subtle that it allows us to interpret each act in context, and this context determines the way we interpret people's behavior.

The number of other ways in which we use our general social intelligence is probably uncountable. We can often tell when a couple has been having an argument. We can tell whether a person is interested in us or finds us attractive. When we are in a crowded store, we can identify which person is the salesclerk just from the person's gaze or facial expression. We usually can recognize the power relationship between two other people who are having a conversation; we can tell which person is the bank president and which is the teller, or which person is the school principal and which is the teacher. Our knowledge on these topics is particularly impressive because of its unconscious nature. We know these things without being able to explain exactly how we know them.

Unique Social Intelligence

I mentioned earlier that each of us possesses two types of social intelligence. So far, we have discussed general social intelligence, the vast store of unconscious knowledge members of a society or culture have in common. The second type of social intelligence results from the sum of our individual backgrounds, lifestyles, and concerns. For this reason, I call this second type *unique social intelligence.* No two people have the same unique social intelligence. This type of knowledge is as individualized as our fingerprints or the details of our autobiographies.

There is another difference between our unique and general social intelligence. Unlike our general social intelligence, our unique social intelligence is not unconscious. We are generally able to identify where this type of knowledge comes from. When we use our unique social intelligence, we tend to be aware that we are using it and also aware of its source.

Because this ability is so individualized, most of my examples of unique social intelligence will be personal. Each of us has examples of this kind, based on our own experiences. My unique social knowledge ranges from different ways of recognizing people to detailed ways of interpreting something about them. One example of my recognition methods concerns cars. I grew up in a lovely small town. Since the word *small* probably means different things to different people, I should say that this town has *one* traffic light. This town was the kind of place where nobody arrived and nobody left—virtually all the students with whom I entered kindergarten graduated from high school together. We lived in a small community, and we all got to know each other over many years.

My family lived outside the town. The window of my second-story room faced the road. Because the town was so small, there wasn't much traffic. But every couple of hours, a car would pass by. If the driver was a friend, he or she would probably honk the horn in a gesture of greeting. When people stopped by and knocked on the front porch door, I could see their cars in the driveway before I could see them at the door.

For these reasons, I learned as a child to identify people by their cars. On the rural roads surrounding the town, I could usually recognize an approaching car when it was still half a mile away. This is an item of unique social intelligence, and I still retain this perceptual habit from my childhood. When I enter the parking lot of my building at the university, I know immediately which other faculty members are parked there. When I go to a party at someone's house, I know before entering the door who the other guests are. Similarly, I can spot a friend in an oncoming car from a considerable distance. I don't know whether other people use this recognition method as much as I do. I do know that when I wave to some friends after recognizing an oncoming car, they look uncertain until they are close enough to recognize my face. I interpret this to mean that most people are "people-recognizers," not "car-recognizers."

Some of these types of unique social intelligence may be splendidly useless. For example, from my own experience, I can usually tell when a man rides a motorcycle. People who drive big bikes usually have a small, precise scuff mark on the top of one boot toe. This is because the toe of the boot is placed under the shift pedal while changing gears. Sometimes I can even tell by this scuff mark what type of bike the person drives. The scuff mark is almost always on the left toe. If it is on the right toe, it usually means that the person drives an older English bike, like a Triumph.

Another example of unique social intelligence is the diagnosis of line behavior. I dislike standing in lines. When choosing among several lines at a fast-food restaurant, I try to stand in the line that I think will move most quickly. As veteran line standers know, there are few things worse than suddenly finding out that the person in front of you is ordering for twenty-seven fellow construction workers or for a busload of kids. My strategy in line prediction is to join any line in which one or more young adults are wearing backpacks.

These people, I have learned, are either students or bicycle riders. Either way, they are almost always ordering for themselves and not for families or groups. This speeds up the line considerably.

One of my favorite areas of unique social intelligence concerns the voice. Recently I had some trouble with my pickup truck. Instead of taking it to my regular garage, I left it with a firm that specializes in wiring problems. When I returned to get the truck a few hours later, the older man who ran the place said, "I couldn't find any shots in the wiring." I looked at him and asked, "Boston?" He smiled broadly and answered, "Fitchburg." My guess was off by a scant thirty-eight miles. The clue, of course, was the pronunciation "shots" instead of "shorts."

Recognizing tourists and people from other nations is for me another item of personal concern. I have always thought it was a simple matter to recognize people traveling outside their native area or society. These people stand out in many ways. Their clothes never look quite "right." Often they carry traveler-type equipment like maps, airline bags, and of course the inevitable cameras. My own strength seems to lie in recognizing British Commonwealth types, perhaps because I have spent some time in both England and New Zealand. On a visit to Yosemite National Park not long ago, I somehow felt sure that a couple seated at the next table in the lodge restaurant was not only Commonwealth but, specifically, English. I am at a loss to explain how I decided this. They hadn't said anything, so I must have relied upon visual clues. There was something overly meticulous about their clothing—for example, the man was wearing a wool suit for his visit to a national park. In addition, the woman's hair was curled up stiffly away from her forehead. Finally, at the risk of using a vague cliché, both their complexions looked ruddy. This description is obviously inadequate, and I may have noticed more details without being conscious of them.

As the meal progressed, I became increasingly confident about my guess. The woman looked horrified when the waiter brought her a pot of hot water and a tea bag. I said to myself, "Definitely English." Finally, unable to stand the suspense, I leaned across the aisle and said, "It's not like English tea, is it?" The woman's eyebrows raised in surprise, and she replied, with national tact, "Well, it's really rather—shall we say—unexpected." We had a nice conversation. It turned out that they were from Yorkshire and were on a ten-day American tour.

We also have unique areas of social intelligence as a result of the work we do. Part of my own work involves giving lectures in large social psychology and sociology classes. This gives me an opportunity to try to read the nonverbal behavior of crowds. I often have the feeling that a specific student is going to raise a hand and ask a question—before he or she actually does it. I think the clues are in facial expressions. Students look puzzled if they do not understand something, or triumphant if they are anxious to score a brilliant point at my expense. Either way, they are likely to raise a hand.

Lecturing has also taught me that entire audiences have perceptible moods. These group emotions include impatience, boredom, disagreement, disinterest, and even (but seldom) inspiration. Each of these reactions is indicated by quite different types of clues. Energetic note-taking usually means that the lecture is going fairly well. When note-taking stops entirely, it means that the lecture is either a miserable failure or a great success. The difference can be read from nonverbal clues. If the lecture is failing, the students are slumped dejectedly in their seats. If the lecture is succeeding, the students sit upright in their seats, lean forward in their chairs, and wear thoughtful expressions on their faces. I think that the "thoughtful" expression consists of a slight lowering of the eyebrows, a pursed look in the mouth, and perhaps touching a finger or pen to the lips.

Because we all have different lives, no two people share the same unique social intelligence. I can, however, try to guess some of the things people know as a result of their work. For example, I am always amazed that the police can arrest someone from a photograph on a wanted poster or even from a description heard over the police radio. I suppose this means that police officers somehow train themselves to be observant about physical descriptions. On the street, of course, there are other clues to work from. They may notice that one person walking on a crowded sidewalk suddenly turns to face a store window as a squad car comes around the corner. Perhaps police officers become good at recognizing "furtive" nonverbal behavior.

It is obviously equally important for people in some professions to be able to recognize the police in or out of uniform. This would be very important for dealers in illegal drugs or for prostitutes. I have heard it said that people in these professions look to see if a man appears to be carrying two wallets in his pants—a normal wallet for public view, and a second wallet containing a badge and other police identification. When I asked a police officer about this, he told me that it might be true for some officers. He said that plainclothes police are required to carry a badge and an I.D. card in addition to any personal papers and money. When I asked him how he managed this, he told me he carried a wallet for his personal items and also a flat leather case for his badge and I.D. card. This would look like two wallets, so perhaps this item of folk social intelligence has some validity.

Every profession requires expertise in certain areas of social intelligence. Clinical psychologists and psychiatrists need to become good at detecting concealed or conflicting feelings. Even when a client or patient claims to feel one way—or neutral—about a certain issue, a good therapist needs to be able to spot signs of concealed emotions. These nonverbal signs may contradict what the person says, but they may be a more accurate indication of the person's feelings than verbal reports. Whether or not most therapists *are* sensitive in this way is, of course, another question. This is clearly a profession in which a keen social intelligence would be extremely valuable.

I suspect that all of us have acquired unique social intelligence abilities from our work. Blackjack dealers need to see through a player's bluff. Store personnel have to be able to spot a shoplifter. A person working on a crisis hotline needs to determine whether the person on the phone is potentially suicidal. Even basketball players need to be able to read the difference between a head fake and a real jump shot.

Unique social intelligence also results from parenting. A parent needs to be able to decode a three-year-old's emotions and the causes of the child's behavior. Parents can sometimes spot a child's unhappiness before the first tears appear, and it is a fine science that allows a parent to know whether a child is angry, hungry, sleepy, bored, or just in need of cuddling. There is evidence that these parenting skills clearly benefit social intelligence. Recent psychological research has shown that parents of young, prelanguage children become extremely sensitive to tone of voice. Tests show that these parents are unusually good at reading nonverbal communication in the voice—even when the speaker is an adult. This shows that the child "teaches" the parent just as the parent teaches the child.

Some people have developed their social intelligence to a high degree, as two final examples will show. I think that both are remarkable demonstrations of social intelligence. The first example comes from my first year of university teaching in 1972. One of my courses was a research seminar on nonverbal communication. This seminar had to be limited to twenty-five undergraduates, but roughly one hundred students applied for admission. When this many people showed up to enroll in the course, I asked the students to write a few paragraphs about their background preparation and their interest in the course. This request produced a serious and earnest statement from almost all the students.

One of the more memorable statements, however, came from a woman who was a college sophomore. She explained her desire to take the course by writing the following:

> Wow, am I jazzed about this course! This seems like the most amazing academic trampoline on campus this quarter and I am dying to bounce on it! This course seems perfect for me since I am nonverbal, nonlinear, and very intense about life right now! This course is a rush!!
>
> Sally Sanders
> (not her real name)

Since I was new to university teaching, I really didn't know what to make of this. I was particularly at a loss, since roughly one hundred students had crowded into the seminar room, and I had no idea what Sally Sanders looked like. I decided to show the statement to a woman friend who has always seemed to me to have a keen social intelligence. She read the statement and examined the florid handwriting and punctuation. Then my friend said, "I think I can guess exactly what she looks like. She is extremely thin. She wears her hair very long and clips it carelessly in back. She wears an ethnic blouse and leaves the top unbuttoned. She wears a white coral necklace and has a ring on every finger of both hands except the thumbs." Well, I thought, anyone can spin a web of imaginary details.

The next day, some of the one hundred students dropped by to see if they had been admitted to the course. As luck would have it, Sally Sanders was one of them. When I opened my office door and heard her name, I realized that I was participating in a great social intelligence episode. Sally Sanders was unmistakably the woman my friend had described. Every detail was confirmed: the thinness, the hair, the partly unbuttoned ethnic blouse, the coral necklace, and even the eight rings on her fingers. Later that day, when I asked my friend how she had constructed her prediction, she could only say, "It was just the way someone who wrote that statement would look."

My second example concerns that undisputed fictional master of social intelligence, Sherlock Holmes. In his autobiography, *Memories and Adventures,* Sir Arthur Conan Doyle revealed that the detective Sherlock Holmes was modeled after an Edinburgh professor of surgery, Dr. Joseph Bell. Doyle had been a medical student under Bell, and he was frequently astonished at the professor's powers of interpretation. As an example, Doyle reports an actual interview between Professor Bell and a patient he has met for the first time. Professor Bell has no clues in this interview except for those he can observe. The encounter is a masterpiece of unique social intelligence.

PROF. BELL: Well my man, you've served in the army?
PATIENT: Aye, Sir.
PROF. BELL: Not long discharged?
PATIENT: No, Sir.
PROF. BELL: A Highland regiment?
PATIENT: Aye, Sir.
PROF. BELL: A non-com officer?
PATIENT: Aye, Sir.
PROF. BELL: Stationed at Barbados?
PATIENT: Aye, Sir.

This exchange demonstrates the powers of deduction with

which Holmes would dazzle the slow-witted Watson in story after story. But the professor was real, not fictional. How could Professor Bell have known all these things about a man he had only just met? One of the students, perhaps Doyle himself, was bold enough to ask this question. In his autobiography, Doyle recalls Professor Bell's explanation:

> "You see, gentlemen," he would explain, "the man was a respectful man but did not remove his hat. They do not in the army, but he would have learned civilian ways had he been long discharged. He has an air of authority and he is obviously Scottish. As to Barbados, his complaint is elephantiasis, which is West Indian, and not British." To his audience of Watsons, it all seemed very miraculous until it was explained, and then it became simple enough.

Improving Social Intelligence

Both general and unique social intelligence are based on a reading of verbal and nonverbal clues. In order to make accurate interpretations about people, we must be able to listen to what they say and also to decode nonverbal clues in their appearance, tone of voice, and interactions with others.

I have mentioned that most of us have difficulty describing nonverbal clues, even though we may recognize their meaning. This is because our understanding of nonverbal clues is learned without being taught to us verbally. These clues are rarely included in a school's curriculum. It is rare for us to discuss these clues with one another, particularly since we seem to use them unconsciously. We learn what we do know about nonverbal clues from our experiences with other people—parents, friends, lovers, and children. Although we use nonverbal clues every time we look at or listen to another person, we tend not to be aware of this level of behavior. Clearly, there is a verbal bias in our culture.

This book attempts to increase our ability to read nonverbal clues and to learn more about social intelligence. To do this, it uses a series of photographs. These pictures were taken in a wide range of settings, and I think they have captured people in natural poses. These photographs were shown to people who were asked to answer a specific social intelligence question about each photograph. These people were also asked to tell us what clues they saw in each photograph. The next chapter explains the plan of this book and describes the taking of these photographs and the construction and testing of the questions.

2 THE PLAN OF THIS BOOK

This book contains a series of social intelligence items consisting of one or more photographs paired with a single question. Several possible answers are given for each question, and only one of these answers is correct. On each item, the reader can try to answer the question before reading about the correct answer. In trying to interpret each of the photographs, you may find that both your general and unique social intelligence are helpful.

The social intelligence items are grouped by topic in different chapters. "Recognizing Intimacy" is about the clues we can use to guess something about the relationship between two people. The next chapter, "Lovers and Strangers," is about recognizing the difference between "real" couples and "fake" couples. Family relationships are discussed in "Kinship Clues," and "Signs of Power and Competition" deals with the clues that reveal the balance of power between two people.

Each of these chapters begins with a discussion of the kinds of social intelligence that might be useful for answering the questions in that chapter. The introduction to the next chapter, for example, concerns the kinds of clues that might help a person to recognize intimacy between two people. A series of social intelligence items is presented next. For each question, the reader is able to see what percent of our male and female judges chose the right answer to this question. This will indicate how easy or difficult each photograph is to read.

I have also summarized the comments these men and women made about each photograph. These comments include their intuitive impressions of the people in each photograph and their opinions about the important clues in each picture. By expanding our awareness of the clues other people see, this information can help us to increase our social intelligence. I should mention that I regard the judges' comments as data, and I have not tampered with them in any way. I have preserved these comments in their original language and grammar, correct or not, simply because I wish to be faithful to what the judges said.

The final chapter of the book, "Improving Your Social Intelligence," outlines a practical method for using everyday experiences to improve social intelligence. This chapter describes ways we can continue to exercise and test our social intelligence in our private and working lives.

Taking the Pictures, Choosing the Questions, and Finding the Judges

In planning the pictures for this book, I was committed to capturing people in their natural surroundings. I did not want to bring people to a studio, psychology lab, or office, because I felt that being in these places would make people pose formally and unnaturally. Since some of the people in this book are friends or acquaintances, it was fairly easy to arrange their photographs in informal settings.

We quickly learned, however, that taking pictures of complete strangers under field conditions is a different matter. On the street, we had to explain to people that we were not (a) trying to sell them snapshots, (b) giving out religious literature, (c) peddling magazine subscriptions, or (d) asking for spare change. We explained that we needed pictures for a study of whether or not people could interpret clues from photographs. The most common response was economic anxiety—many people asked whether it would cost them anything to be photographed. Once reassured on this point, most people were extremely helpful. Sometimes, people approached us and asked to be photographed when they saw that we were taking pictures.

A number of photographs may appear out of focus or improperly exposed, or have imperfections of some kind. Because of our requirements, we could not shoot these pictures over. They are included because they are the photographs that were used with the questions, and they do demonstrate points about social intelligence.

In choosing people to be photographed, we wanted to maximize diversity. We tried to include men and women of all ages, many occupations, and most ethnic groups. No informal sample can be perfectly representative, of course, and ours is no exception. Our pictures were all taken in California, but I think they provide a reasonable cross section of the diverse population of this large state.

With a few exceptions, the pictures we took show people as we found them. They knew, of course, that they were being photographed, so many of the people are shown facing the camera. In almost all other ways, the photographs are entirely natural. People are shown in the clothes they were wearing, and in most cases, they are shown next to the person or people we found them with. The exception to these guidelines is that we sometimes asked two strangers to stand next to each other and to pretend that they were a real couple.

Once the pictures were taken and printed, a social intelligence question was written for each one. These questions are in a multiple-choice format with two or three possible answers. For example, a picture of a man and woman might be paired with the following multiple-choice question: These two people are: (a) a couple, (b) strangers, or (c) brother and sister.

In designing these questions, I tried to follow three guidelines. First, I wanted to make the questions interesting, since an uninteresting or trivial question is probably not worth asking. Second, I wanted every question to be realistic—to be the kind of social intelligence question that we might encounter in real life. Third, I wanted every question to have a "right" or objectively correct answer.

This last point is important. Many types of questions do not have objective answers. For example, suppose someone shows you a photograph of a woman's face and asks you, "Is this woman sad?" Unfortunately there is no way of knowing what the right answer to this question really is. How could we ever *know*—in some absolute sense—whether the woman was sad or not? If a person tells us he or she is sad, do we always take the person's word for this? If the person denies being sad, do we always accept this at face value? Questions like this also suffer from problems of definition. Sadness over losing a tennis game obviously differs from sadness over losing a spouse. Which of these emotions are we looking for in the face of the woman in this example? There are many other types of subjective or unanswerable questions, such as "Is this a nice person?" "Does this man enjoy music?" and "Does this woman love her husband?" I have avoided subjective and debatable questions of this kind.

Finally, once the photographs had been printed and the questions written, we needed a population of judges to determine whether the questions could be answered. We managed to find a total of twenty-four hundred willing judges on or near three campuses of the University of California: Berkeley, Santa Cruz, and Los Angeles. The judges we tested on each campus were mainly undergraduates at these universities. The other judges were students contacted at smaller colleges or people we met in nearby parks and other locations.

Each judge was asked to answer about fifteen social intelligence items and to tell us what he or she thought were the significant clues in each photograph. This took roughly twenty minutes. We explained to each judge that we were studying the ways in which people interpret photographs. We also told them, truthfully, that we were interested in how well each picture could be read and not in how "good" or "accurate" each person was as a judge. Finally, we explained that there were no tricks and that each of the questions had an objectively correct answer.

Most of our judges were extremely interested in the project, and they became enthusiastic as soon as we explained the nature of the study. This was not true of all judges, however. It seems that psychology has only a mixed reputation for honesty. Several judges asked us what the study was "really" about. A few judges said they thought it was a secret psychological test for homosexual tendencies, virginity, or neurosis. These suspicions are an unhappy comment on the image of psychological research. It seemed to help our credibility if the research was described as sociological rather than psychological. When told that I was a sociologist, one initially suspicious judge brightened and said, "Oh, then there really *are* right answers!"

What Is Missing from This Book

Some things have been left out of this book for ethical reasons. This is important because this book uses photographs of real people, not actors, and because some of the social intelligence questions involve highly personal information. Some of the topics we omitted probably would have made interesting social intelligence questions. I could have constructed questions about which one of two people in a photograph was an alcoholic, a prostitute, a convicted murderer, or an ex-patient in a psychiatric facility. A great many questions of this kind could have been constructed, and I believe that we sometimes make interpretations of this kind in real life. However, since these photographs were going to be made public, along with the correct answer to each question, I decided that it was ethically unacceptable to expose people to potential embarrassment or stigma.

Many people volunteered to pose for photographs that would involve sensitive questions of this kind. For example, several people volunteered to be photographed to see whether judges could guess that they were homosexual. One gay woman was willing to have judges guess which of two people—herself or another woman—was the lesbian. These people seemed to be motivated by the belief that prejudice against homosexuals would be reduced if they were less secretive and more visible.

This posed something of a dilemma for me. Since a question of this kind ("Which of these two women says she is a lesbian?") would be interesting, I would have liked to include it in the book. In addition, these people had read and signed consent forms that clearly described the use of the photographs. Because of the sensitive nature of the topic, I asked these people to take some time to reflect on their decisions. Some weeks later, I asked them to make the decision all over again. They were still willing, and they signed a second, more detailed consent form. By any professional standard, I believe that these precautions fulfilled my formal ethical obligations as a researcher. I also discussed the matter with several colleagues, and they all seemed to think I should use the material.

For several reasons, however, I was not comfortable with this decision. It did not seem ethical to me to accept a consent given in someone's youth that would be binding on the person's future. What would happen, I wondered, if some of these people changed their lifestyle in later life and regretted this youthful disclosure? Even though no names were to be used, people obviously could be recognized from their photographs. Book publication would make these disclosures permanent as well as public.

I felt that there were also other risks, and some of these were not at all vague or uncertain. At the time these young Californians were granting their consent for this disclosure, they knew that voters in their state were considering a ballot measure that would allow school boards to fire teachers who practiced, admitted, or even advocated homosexuality. The dangers of admitting homosexuality, therefore, were not at all hypothetical. Since some of these people might want to become teachers, I could not understand why they were willing to take such great personal risks. Ultimately, it became a personal decision for me. I simply decided that I did not want to help people to take risks of this magnitude. For this reason, this material was never used.

Something else is also missing from the book. I have "censored" certain kinds of comments made by some judges about some of the people in the photographs. This affects a very small number of comments. Our twenty-four hundred judges made over thirty thousand individual comments, and no more than two hundred of these have been censored. I decided not to report these two hundred comments because they seemed to be particularly malicious. Since people put themselves on the line by agreeing to have the pictures made public, it seems to me that this courage earns them the right to be protected from pointlessly hurtful remarks. In addition, these destructive remarks were clearly in the minority. Only a few judges seemed interested in a "put-down" style of analysis that concentrated on the physical appearance and presumed intelligence or character of the subjects.

There is another reason for not reporting these reactions. Some of these evaluations are quite debatable, and it doesn't seem fair to allow them to go uncontradicted. For example, one judge made a nasty comment about a supposedly "homely" couple. I thought both these people were very attractive, and so did several other people. Finally, there is no scientific reason to report these negative comments. The nondestructive comments are more fascinating and instructive, as will become clear in succeeding chapters.

3 RECOGNIZING INTIMACY

How do we recognize intimacy? What are the significant clues that tell us two people are in love? How can we tell if two people are lovers or merely friends? Do these clues change as a relationship ages? Can we tell how long two people have been a couple by the way they treat one another? These are some of the questions this chapter will explore.

Love and intimacy are important experiences in life, and we have all seen their impact on others' lives as well as our own. As a result, this is one area of social intelligence where folk theories abound. Early in the movie *Two for the Road,* for example, Audrey Hepburn and Albert Finney are considering marriage. While seated in a restaurant, they notice that all the unmarried lovers in the restaurant talk to each other and visibly enjoy one another's presence. The married couples, by contrast, sit silent. Hepburn and Finney conclude, rather dismally, that this is how one can recognize a married couple.

As far as I know, this folk theory of marriage has not been tested scientifically. One could, I suppose, spend several days in restaurants recording the sheer volume of conversation between each couple. Then, as each couple left, an interviewer could ask them whether or not they are married. The Hepburn-Finney hypothesis would be supported if it turned out that the unmarried people had talked during their meal, while the married people had not. Even if the married people had not talked, of course, it could be due simply to how long they had been together or even their age. Perhaps people talk less as they grow older. The best test of the

Hepburn-Finney hypothesis would be a comparison of married and unmarried people who were all the same age and "together" for the same length of time.

Whether or not this hypothesis is true, it is one of several interesting folk theories about intimacy. According to these theories, we can decode the relationship between two people using a number of specific clues. There are many folk theories about which clues are significant. One of my favorites is something I call the "front-seat-distance hypothesis." It proposes that the intensity of the "new love" between two people varies inversely with the distance separating them as they drive. People who have been married for a long time tend to sit next to a car's windows, far from one another. When a man and a woman are young and very much in love, however, they tend to sit as close to one another as is physically possible.

A number of automotive innovations have probably made the front-seat-distance hypothesis less dramatic than it once was. Individual or bucket seats, seat belts, and swivel chairs like those now offered in vans all limit a couple's freedom to arrange themselves on the seats of many current automobiles. Despite these innovations, the front-seat-distance hypothesis still seems valid. Young couples can be seen sitting side by side behind the wheel, while older couples seldom show this signal of intimacy.

There are other folk theories about how to recognize intimacy. A friend of mine says that he has never known a new or unmarried couple in which the man or woman reads a newspaper during a meal. This observation is similar to the Hepburn-Finney hypothesis. Both observations reflect the belief that young or unmarried lovers have an especially intense relationship—one that is so exciting and absorbing that it leaves little time for either bored silences or the daily newspapers. The signs of this intensity are the clues that can enable us to be socially intelligent about the relationship between two people.

Psychologists and sociologists have recently become interested in studying clues of this kind. Psychologist Nancy Henley has studied patterns of touching, particularly male-female differences in public touching behavior. For example, Henley has identified a "gesture of power." When two people interact, the higher status person can put an arm around the shoulder of the lower status person. It almost never happens that people put their arms around someone who is higher in status than themselves. The president of a bank can put an arm around the bank's vice-president as they walk down a hall, but the reverse is almost unthinkable. Henley has also found that this same power gesture seems to operate between men and women. Men sometimes hold women in this way, but the reverse is extremely rare.

Sociologist Erving Goffman has also studied male and female gestures. He agrees with Henley that men tend to use this "shoulder hold," but he thinks it can indicate other qualities in addition to power—support, protection, goodwill, or affection. Goffman agrees with Henley that men use the shoulder hold more often, and he says that men use it with women if no intimacy is involved in the relationship.

When real intimacy is involved, however, Goffman says the way people touch in public changes dramatically. When two people are really a couple, it is the woman who enjoys an almost unlimited touching privilege. Goffman calls this the woman's "license to touch." The woman in a couple is freer to touch the man in public than he is to touch her. For example, when they are casually seated together, the woman may rest her hand on the man's knee or even on his thigh. It is extremely unusual for a man to touch a woman in public in this manner, even if they are married or lovers. Goffman says this is because in our culture the woman's touch is not thought to be sexual in intent. Men cannot touch women in this manner because such touching would be seen as sexually motivated and therefore improper in public.

The theories we have discussed so far have concerned the way people behave. Other theories involve the way people look. Some focus on formal symbols of romantic availability. The ability to recognize these symbols is most important to a person who wants to become involved with a new person, but I believe that all of us are broadcasting clues about whether or not we are "available," whatever our personal situations. For example a woman friend once told me that whenever she met a man for the first time she would, almost without thinking, check to see if he wore anything on the ring finger of his left hand.

Other symbols of availability can be equally revealing—a man or woman pushing a stroller, the presence of jars of baby food in someone's shopping basket, or the type of personal photographs displayed in a wallet or on a person's desk. Even the type of trash in the back seats of cars can reveal something about one's availability; pacifiers, nipples from bottles, parts from building-block sets, beach toys, or athletic equipment reveal the presence of children of specific ages. All of these clues can be read by the observant or socially intelligent person.

There are other clues in a person's appearance. For example, I know a woman who claims she can readily recognize mothers of young children. She says they commonly have food stains and other markings on their clothing. Another woman told me she can identify when a young woman is unattached by her clothes. Single women, she says, spend conspicuously more money on clothes than do married women of the same age. This friend said that while single women do not necessarily dress more "provocatively," their appearance does reflect a larger investment of time, care, and money.

According to some folk theories, even the shape of a person's body can provide important clues. There is a common belief that people "let themselves go" when they have found a mate. A few years after marriage, according to this theory, both men and women gain weight. There are some fascinating variations on this weight hypothesis. I know a man who has a theory that weight can be a valuable clue to the relationship between two people. This person says that two unmarried people can both be thin or both be heavy, since in either case they are matched. As my friend rather coldly puts it, "Fat goes with fat, skinny with skinny." When one member of a couple is thin and the other is heavy, however, my friend says the two people are in every case married because an "imbalance" of this kind would prevent voluntary attraction between two unmarried people.

Some of the most subtle clues to availability involve interaction. Without realizing it, all of us know how to discourage or encourage another person without saying a word. We can send these silent messages in many types of situations. Several years ago, some friends and I attended a postal auction in Boston and came away with hundreds of paperback books that had been lost in the mails. These were new books on a variety of topics. We decided to try to give away the extra books on a downtown Boston street to test the widespread belief that people will not accept free money or gifts from strangers on the street. We found that only about one person in three would accept a book, and some people gave marvelous explanations for not taking one: "I'm only visiting Boston," "I already have a book at home," "I collect coins," and "My wife makes the decisions."

The most interesting thing about this street experiment was that people gave very different types of silent signals when they saw our two book givers, even when they were hundreds of feet away. People who did not want to talk with us or find out what we were doing used their bodies to give us the message that they did not want to get involved. As they walked toward us, these people carefully looked away—at the pavement, at their watches, or at store windows. They also leaned forward sharply as they approached, and the angle of their bodies gave us the message that they were in a hurry and did not wish to be bothered.

Signals about romantic availability are different from avoidance signals. One such signal is merely being in a certain place at a certain time—being alone at a bar frequented by single people may be read as a signal that you are available. Other signals have to do with subtle aspects of behavior. One of these signals is eye contact. At times all of us may stare at an attractive person who is a stranger to us. The social rules regarding staring are, however, quite strict. If a person looks at us and catches us staring at him or her, we almost always look away. It is embarrassing in our culture to be caught staring at another person.

When we bend or break this social rule, it may be read as a desire for involvement with a person. Even if we are caught staring, we may boldly decide to stare again a minute later. When the person catches us staring, we may hold eye contact for a daring half-second longer than the social rules allow, to communicate our interest. The other person "answers" our silent message in one of two ways. Unavailability or disinterest is eloquently communicated by simply refusing to acknowledge our eye contact. Availability can be signaled by returning our gaze. This returned eye contact is so unusual and laden with meaning that it constitutes the famous "lingering look," although I doubt this type of eye contact among strangers ever "lingers" for more than a second.

Mutual eye contact can sometimes lead to embarrassing misunderstandings. I was once in a bar with the other members of a rather inept basketball team—the season was half over and I believe we were celebrating our first win. Five or six of us were seated at a table, drinking beer and savoring our victory. There were several young women at the next table, and after a minute or so, I became aware that one of the women was staring at me. I looked in her direction, expecting her to look away immediately. She did not look away. Instead, she held eye contact for at least a second, and I was the one who finally blushed and looked away. Then, gazing discreetly at my glass of beer, I tried to think what this flagrant violation of the eye contact rules could mean. I tried out four hypotheses in my mind: (1) perhaps this was someone I had met but did not recognize, like a former student in a large lecture class; (2) perhaps she had lost her glasses and could not tell that I had established eye contact with her; (3) perhaps she was in an altered state of consciousness in which I looked like a potted plant to her; or (4) perhaps she was really encouraging me to try to pick her up.

At that moment, as I puzzled to myself, the mystery was dissolved. One of the men at my table leaned forward and said in a whisper, "Hey, see those women at the next table? They're prostitutes—they're in this bar every night." I made a mental note that he had not explained how *he* happened to know they were in that bar every night. He did say that the woman who stared at me had approached a friend of his and was bold enough to name the price of an evening in her company. My fourth hypothesis, therefore, was not far wrong—the woman was in fact signaling her availability. Although I could tell she was breaking all the rules for discreet eye contact, I had not guessed that her interest in me was entrepreneurial rather than romantic. How humbling!

In some situations, we have only incomplete clues when we try to interpret the relationship between two people. For example, if we observe a man and a much younger woman at a table on the other side of a crowded restaurant, we may try to guess what their relationship is. Are they lovers, a married couple, co-workers, or father and daughter? If we cannot overhear their conversation, we may have to rely on whether they hold hands and how, whether they stare at each other, and other types of visual clues.

We are in a similar situation when we see only fragments or "slices" of behavior. I was once driving behind a car in which the driver and passenger appeared to be gesturing wildly. At first I thought they were having a spectacular argument, but when I stopped behind them at a light, I realized that at least one of the people was deaf. What I thought was an argument was simply the use of hands in an animated "sign" conversation.

We frequently are exposed to partial clues of this kind. One of the most common examples is when we happen to be in a room while someone else is using the telephone. Overhearing someone else's phone call is one of the very best natural "test items" of social intelligence. Since we can observe only half of the conversation, we are presented with a perfect opportunity to make several guesses about the person we cannot hear or see. We can try to guess the sex and age of the person and how the person we can hear feels about the other person. When the conversation is finished, we can ask the person with us whether or not our guesses are accurate.

As part of a study of nonverbal communication, Robin Akert and I once videotaped a young woman as she made a telephone call. Then we selected part of her telephone call and made a record of it in two different ways. One was simply the videotape of the telephone call. The second record was just a written transcript of her part of the conversation. We gave these two versions of the phone call to two different groups of college students and asked them to try to guess whether the woman had been talking to a man or to a woman. One group of students saw a short videotape, and the other group saw only the transcript of the woman's half of the conversation. Can you predict which of the two groups made more accurate guesses?

Here is the transcript of the woman's half of the conversation:

Oh, well, you can't go because I have . . . You know . . . So . . . Well, 'cause . . . Yeah . . . Yeah . . . Oh, you know . . . Just awhile . . . Well, because I just had to, you know . . . Yeah, yeah . . . I think you can do it.

The college students who saw only this transcript were split almost evenly in their guesses about the sex of the other person; 51 percent of the students guessed it was a man, and 49 percent guessed it was a woman. One of the students, a woman who guessed that the other person was a woman, said, "The woman is too assertive to be talking to a man . . . Women aren't conditioned to talk like that to a man, and if she was (talking to a man) all of her other words would have been more carefully chosen."

In this book I cannot show you the videotape of the woman's phone call, but here is a single photograph taken from the videotape.

The students who saw the videotape of the telephone call answered very differently. Eighty-seven percent of these students guessed that the woman was talking to a man, and they were right. The woman on the phone was talking to a man, and almost nine out of ten people were able to recognize this easily. One of the students commented, "She is saying no with an intensely fond smile. It's probably a man she likes." Another student said, "She laughed like she was talking to a man." A third student said, "She's talking to a man. The casting down of her eyes is a coy courting mannerism."

This example shows that social intelligence requires the ability to read nonverbal clues. Our students were not able to get the right answer when they were shown only the verbal clues in the transcript. The students who used both verbal and nonverbal clues in the videotape did dramatically better. The videotape provided the nonverbal context that is absolutely necessary for an understanding of the spoken word. Facial expressions, eye movements, gestures, and tone of voice provide a nonverbal script that adds life to words. This nonverbal script enables us to understand the real meaning of what a person says. Social intelligence requires more than verbal clues. It consists of the ability to interpret what a person says in light of the "symphony" of nonverbal acts that accompanies these words.

The ability to recognize intimacy—to interpret the nature of the relationship between two people—is clearly an important part of social intelligence. We have taken photographs of large numbers of couples, and these photographs are shown in this chapter and in chapter 4. The photographs in this chapter show people exactly as our photographers found them. Some of the photographs in chapter 4, however, show "fake" couples—strangers who agreed to pose together for us. In both chapters, the photographs can provide clues to the relationship between two people. A photograph provides a "slice" of nonverbal behavior that shows two people in a single moment in their relationship. Although photographs provide fewer clues than an hour-long videotape, we have learned that they frequently contain extremely accurate clues about a relationship.

In this chapter people are shown as our camera found them. All the photographs were taken in field settings—on the street, in offices, in stores, in restaurants, in parks, and at the beach. Each picture is paired with a question. After we had photographed a person or a couple, we asked them for the kinds of details we would need to construct a social intelligence question for this picture. In the case of couples, we asked the two people what their relationship was, how long they had known each other, whether they were married, and so on.

What is the best strategy for answering the social intelligence questions? I think the best method is to look carefully at each picture. Try to see which answer seems to be the best "fit" for each picture. Remember that there are no tricks—we did not try to find any pictures that were deliberately misleading. On the basis of looking at some of the pictures, you may feel you can eliminate certain answers. For other pictures, you may have a vague sense that one of the answers is correct, even if you cannot explain this impression. The most useful guide in answering the questions will probably be your own intuitive social intelligence. Try to answer each question before looking ahead to see the correct answer. This approach requires you to work at reading each picture, but I think it is more likely to improve your interpretive abilities.

Each picture and question was tested with about two hundred people—roughly one hundred women and one hundred men. The judges' answers and comments are summarized in two ways. The accuracy of their answers is indicated by three percentages. The first percentage shows how many women chose the right answer, the second shows how many men chose this answer, and the third is a total percentage showing how many female and male judges were right.

The guessing or "chance" accuracy level also is given. This will help to show how easy or difficult each question is. The chance accuracy level is a rough estimate of how well people would do by random guessing. This chance accuracy level is a function of the number of multiple-choice alternatives for each question. A question with two alternatives has a chance accuracy level of 50 percent. Half the people should get the right answer to this question merely by guessing. Questions with three alternatives have a chance accuracy level of 33.3 percent; only one person in three should get the right answer by guessing alone.

It is a simple matter to tell how difficult each question is. For example, if a question has three possible answers, the chance accuracy level is 33.3 percent. But if 52 percent of the women and 58 percent of the men get the right answer, we can conclude that these people did much better than chance. This indicates that this photograph is fairly easy—that it does in fact "contain" the kinds of useful clues that are necessary for socially intelligent interpretations. You can use this information to compare the difficulty of different questions.

Finally, I have summarized what our judges said about each picture and the people in it. These comments are a valuable tool for improving your social intelligence. They make it possible for you to compare what you "see" in each photograph with the clues detected by our judges. The judges' comments allow us to share in the perceptions, insights, and unique social intelligence of this diverse group of people. After you have had a chance to look at all the photographs in this chapter, there is a brief conclusion about the recognition of intimacy.

What is the relationship between these two people?

    a. husband and wife

    b. student and teacher

    c. close friends

Answer: b. student and teacher

Accuracy (33.3%)

Women	Men	Total
97.0%	94.0%	95.5%

This was one of the "easiest" photographs in our study. Better than nine out of ten judges correctly identified the relationship between the two people as that of student and teacher. Some people used environmental props as clues; many judges cited the blackboard in the background and the pencil in the man's hand.

There were many interaction cues as well. The two people are standing farther apart than one would expect of either close friends or a husband and wife. Many judges were struck by the people's facial expressions and body positions. One judge cited the "cold practicality of their looks." Several judges thought the most important clues were the crossed arms. Judges said the man seems to be instructing, and the woman seems to be defensive.

One female judge even invented a small scenario: "The man on the right (the teacher) is explaining to the woman (the student) why she didn't pass her midterm exam. Her arms are folded in self-defense." As a university faculty member, I must say that I cringe at this description—are student-teacher relations really so combative? I suppose, however, that 95 percent of our judges can't be wrong.

These two people have known each other for:

    a. an hour

    b. a year

    c. five years

Answer: a. an hour

Accuracy (33.3%)

Women	Men	Total
56.4%	65.1%	60.6%

There is no real intimacy in this photograph, and 60 percent of our judges were able to recognize this fact. These two people were introduced just prior to our taking this photograph. Most of our judges commented on two specific clues: the distance between the man and woman, and their smiles. One male judge commented that they are standing too far apart to be anything but strangers, and he said "they look somewhat uneasy—the bodies seem rigid." A woman said the two people look "like strangers greeting each other." The smiles in this picture seemed unconvincing or merely polite to our judges. One man said the two people look "a little unsure about how the other person is reacting to them." Other judges said the smiles were "cold" or "forced," and one man said simply, "They are faking it."

The faces provided additional information. One woman said that the two people "do not appear to know each other extremely well—there is a look of questioning, uncertainty, and curiosity on both faces." Several people were struck by the direction of the man's gaze. He is not making eye contact with the woman and in fact seems to be looking *over* her head. Several people thought this lack of eye contact indicated a "superficial" relationship.

The two people in this picture may have been trying to act warm and friendly, but the nonverbal pieces just did not fit together in a convincing manner. This is summarized by one woman judge: "Considering the fact that they aren't looking straight at each other, the smiles come off as a bit forced. They probably were put together by the photographer." She was right.

These two people:

      a. have just met for the first time a few hours ago

      b. have known each other for four years and are in
         love

      c. are brother and sister

Answer: b. have known each other for four years and are in love

Accuracy (33.3%)

Women	Men	Total
85.9%	**75.0%**	**80.6%**

Over 80 percent of our judges correctly identified the loving relationship between these two people. Accuracy was even higher among women judges. The judges' comments clearly show that the picture is an eloquent portrait of intimacy.

This picture contains precisely the kind of natural eye contact one rarely sees between strangers. Most of our judges commented on the significance of this special way of looking. One woman was struck by "the way they look at each other and are smiling *at* each other, as if they share some deep inner secret that's special." Another woman said, "They have complete understanding and happiness in their eyes—they look like they really know each other." Most judges also had no trouble recognizing that this intimacy was different from the affection one might find between brother and sister. For example, one judge said, "The exchange of glances is very powerful and giving. . . ."

Several judges commented on the fact that the man and woman are touching. One said, "They are looking at each other and being physically affectionate with each other like lovers." One judge seemed carried away by the romantic qualities of this photograph. She said, "They are holding each other. They are looking directly at one another. They are smiling, and there is a tilt to their heads. If they came a foot closer together, they would be kissing." Clearly this photograph has captured some of the intimacy and love that exists between these two people.

This couple is married. They have known each other:

    a. nine months

    b. nine years

    c. thirty-nine years

Answer: c. thirty-nine years

Accuracy (33.3%)

Women	Men	Total
67.7%	**63.3%**	**65.5%**

About two thirds of our judges recognized that this couple had been together for a very long time. A few judges incorrectly thought this relationship was younger, apparently because they do not expect people who have been married for a long time to be quite as happy as these two people appear to be. Some judges, who guessed that these people had been married only nine months, said, "They look like happy honeymooners," "They are still smiling," and "They look too happy to be married a long time." A judge who guessed they had been married nine years explained his answer by saying, "There is still a spark in the relationship." These comments say more about some of our judges' dim views of marriage than they do about the people in this photograph.

Some of the other comments about this photograph are related to another theory about intimacy. A number of judges based their decisions on a "matching theory" of couples. This theory says that people are—other things being equal—likely to be attracted to those who are similar or matched in age, appearance, "build," dress, attractiveness, and apparent lifestyle. The basic idea behind matching theory is that we are likely to form a couple with someone who is our "equal" in terms of desirability. One of my favorite definitions of matching theory was given by sociologist Erving Goffman. According to Goffman, marriage occurs in our society when a man suggests to a woman that his assets are not so inferior to hers as to preclude the possibility of a merger.

Many of our judges thought that this photograph captures a special aspect of matching theory. In addition to predicting who will be attracted to whom, matching theory suggests that the "match" between two people will increase as the years pass. One woman judge said, "They say people start to look like each other after many years—these two look just like each other." Another woman said,

"They really seem incredibly alike—same grin, same eye squint, etc. They have adopted each other's characteristics over the years." Most people thought that this kind of visual blending takes a long time. One judge said, "They have a grown-together look about them, and that takes thirty years."

These two people are:

       a. strangers who never met before

       b. brother and sister

       c. a married couple

Answer: b. brother and sister

Accuracy (33.3%)

Women	Men	Total
53.8%	53.7%	53.8%

I like to think of this photograph as a modern version of the famous painting *American Gothic* by Grant Wood. More than half of our judges got the right answer. How did they know that these two people are brother and sister? Many judges cited what they thought was a striking physical resemblance. One man said that these people have similar "hair type," "carriage," and "body and facial structure." A woman judge said these two people have "identical noses and mouths." Some judges even cited similar expressions. One judge said, "They have the same tense smile," and another judge said "their lips are pressed" in the same way.

Many of our judges noticed more subtle details as well. For these judges, the most important thing about the photograph was that the two people seemed to know one another, but there was not the slightest trace of romantic love. The absence of any signs of intimacy was noted by most judges—only 11 percent thought that these two were a married couple. One woman judge said the two people are "not thrilled about standing next to each other," and another woman commented that the two "are not hugging as a couple would." A man said that the "neutral expressions" indicated that there is no romantic closeness between the two. One man gave this imaginative description: "She looks like she is thinking, 'Of all the men in the world, why a guy with his sleeves rolled up like a hard hat?'"

Our judges could tell, however, that the man and woman were not strangers. One woman said, "When strangers are photographed together, it seems they are 'giggly' from being ill at ease with one another. This couple seems to be used to being together." One man said, "They are standing too close to be strangers. But their pose is too formal for a married couple." Several people thought the formality of the pose was an important clue, and one man said, "They do not seem to be emotional about being close together. Looks somewhat like a serious family portrait—he also seems concerned to get his racket in the picture." Finally, one woman said the two are "not entirely disinterested in each other, but they are certainly not young lovers."

The man with the beard is in both photographs. In one he is with a friend he has known for seventeen years; in the other he has known the person less than a week. Which person has he known longer?

       a. the man

       b. the woman

Answer: a. the man

Accuracy (50.0%)

Women	Men	Total
72.0%	77.6%	74.8%

Most of our judges got this question right. This photograph captures a different kind of intimacy than we have seen in earlier photographs—the intimacy bred by an old and strong friendship. Our judges were most impressed by the great sense of ease and trust that exists between the two men. One male judge said, "The bearded man is much more at ease with the man—he isn't embarrassed to take off his glasses." Another man said, "He seems much more casual with the man; he seems to have a more open look, whereas he seems more concerned with his image in the picture with the woman." My favorite comment was made by a woman judge. She said that the two men "look like they are getting a kick out of it—like they can add this to the many experiences they have had." She also said that the man and woman "look like they are getting a kick out of it, but she looks as if she is wondering, 'What is this?'—like she is not totally at ease."

If there is a single, powerful clue in this photograph, it appears to be the friend's arm. Many of our judges commented that this kind of embrace or hug is extremely unusual between men. This observation was in every case made by female judges. One woman said, "Men rarely embrace as warmly unless they know each other well." A second woman called it a "superfriendly pose for guys," and a third woman said, "I think that guys who haven't known each other that long would feel less comfortable being so close together." Finally, another woman offered a variation on this analysis: "American men are usually embarrassed to hug unless they are old buddies or drunk, and they're sober."

I was distressed to see that a few judges chose the man as the longtime friend simply because of a dim view of male-female relationships. One woman said, "Buddies are forever," and another woman concluded glumly that "girls and guys have very *transient* relationships nowadays—it looks like a date." One jaded man explained his answer by saying, "It is almost impossible to know a girl such a long time." Is it?

Picture 1

Picture 2

The same man is in both pictures. In one, he is seated with his wife; in the other, he is seated with an old friend. Which picture shows the husband and wife?

        a. Picture 1

        b. Picture 2

Answer: b. Picture 2

Accuracy (50.0%)

Women	Men	Total
60.0%	64.5%	62.4%

This is not an easy question, but judges still pick the "real" wife by almost a two-to-one margin. Some of the judges who correctly chose Picture 2 used a subtle version of matching theory. They were struck by the remarkable symmetry in Picture 2. One man said that these people were "holding their heads in a sympathetic joint pose—they've been working together for a while." Several judges commented on the "togetherness" and "sameness" of the people in this picture, and one woman referred to the similarity in "attitude."

The judges' decisions were also based on what they thought of the smile of the woman in Picture 1. Some judges were misled by this smile. One man thought this smile indicated that the people were relaxed, and he incorrectly guessed that the smiling woman is the man's wife. Most judges, however, read this smile very differently. A woman said, "In Picture 1, they have smiles that take an effort; in Picture 2, they both seem at ease." Another woman said that the smiling people in Picture 1 "look kind of shy," while the unsmiling people in Picture 2 "look very comfortable together." A third woman said of the real husband and wife in Picture 2, "It looks like it's no big deal whether they are smiling or not."

I am not sure what to make of another woman's comment. She correctly identified the married couple and said, "I find that over the years couples do not smile as much." Does this woman mean that long-term couples are so relaxed that they do not need to smile politely, or that after many years of marriage they have nothing left to smile about?

Several other judges perceptively noticed other things about the unsmiling wife. One man said of the real wife, "She seems to be serenely content with their relationship." Another man said she looked positively "smug," but I like the interpretation of the woman who thought the wife was the woman who "looks like she's proud of him."

These two people are:

    a. brother and sister

    b. a couple married four years

    c. strangers who have just met

Answer: a. brother and sister

Accuracy (33.3%)

Women	Men	Total
51.5%	44.0%	47.8%

Only 5 percent of our judges thought that the two people in this photograph were strangers. The judges thought the two people looked far too familiar with each other to be strangers. One man said the important clue was that the man and woman were "not uncomfortable in very close proximity to each other," and a woman commented on "their physical ease."

The difficult decision for our judges was whether these two were brother and sister or a married couple. Many judges said they detected a strong physical resemblance between the two. Judges mentioned hair texture and color, style of glasses, and type of smile. One judge said that "the chin, forehead, and eyebrow placement look alike." There were also other more subtle clues that the two were siblings. One man said, "She's leaning on him in a nonamorous fashion." One of the shortest explanations was given by a woman who said simply, "They're buddies, not lovers."

This woman is talking:

       a. to a woman who is her boss

       b. to a man friend of three weeks

       c. with an eleven-year-old boy whom she is baby-sitting

Answer: b. to a man friend of three weeks

Accuracy (33.3%)

Women	Men	Total
67.0%	64.3%	65.7%

Two thirds of our judges guessed that the woman is talking to a man friend, although the only available clues are in her face. The judges were impressed not only by the fact that she is smiling, but by the kind of smile. One man said the woman has "a realistic smile, a certain smile, a flirting smile—not a fake smile (to a boss), and not a motherly smile (to a child)." A woman described her expression as a "joyous, flirtatious, sensual, sex-appealish smile."

Many of our judges said this woman was obviously enjoying herself. One female judge said the woman shows "a certain glow," and a man said, "She's happy, animated, slightly embarrassed— her eyes look like she's trying to make an impression." Another judge described her expression as an "almost shy, embarrassed look." It seems to me that all of these clues reflect the observation that this woman is talking to someone she apparently likes, someone to whom she is attracted and who is important to her.

These two people are married and have known each other for:

    a. six months

    b. six years

    c. sixteen years

Answer: b. six years

Accuracy (33.3%)

Women	Men	Total
62.9%	70.5%	66.7%

Exactly two thirds of our judges guessed correctly that these people have known each other for six years. There seem to be several clues that point toward this conclusion, and some of them involve different forms of matching theory.

Many judges thought this relationship could not possibly be either six months or sixteen years old. A woman said, "They look comfortable together, but are not old enough for sixteen years." One man said, "They are young and are close, *but not too close* to each other physically." He may have meant that two people who had been together for only six months would be clinging to each other or showing more intensity. Other judges decided that these two had been together longer than six months because of their "similarity in dress," and the fact that "they seem to know each other's habits." Some judges said the two people looked "very settled" and "relaxed and secure." My favorite comment was made by the woman who thought the two people looked relaxed, but noted, "They haven't yet got the comfortable 'he or she will always be there' look."

A few judges were misled by the apparent happiness of these two people and incorrectly concluded that they had known one another only six months. Three who made this mistake were influenced by the "amorous" look, the "pleased and happy" expressions, and the "freshness" of the couple. One young man, obviously jaded about the prospects of marriage, explained his incorrect answer by saying, "In six years, they won't be smiling." I certainly hope this judge will be pleasantly surprised himself.

These two people are:

    a. a couple married eight years

    b. friends but not a couple

    c. strangers posing together

Answer: b. friends but not a couple

Accuracy (33.3%)

Women	Men	Total
56.8%	55.8%	56.3%

Almost all of our judges could tell that these two were not strangers—fewer than 13 percent chose this answer. One man said they looked "too close and comfortable for strangers," and a woman said, "They pose as if they've done it *many* times before."

But how did our judges know these people were friends and not a couple? One woman said, "They look like they're having a great time together, but they're not in love." A man explained his decision by saying that there is something "nonsexual" about the way they are standing together. Another man said the two looked "relaxed, rather than serious and committed."

Again, some of our more cynical judges said the two people appeared to be too happy to be married. One man said, "No couple smiles like that after eight years." However, 31 percent of our judges thought, incorrectly, that they were married. One woman said, "They seem to be two people who would be attracted to each other." I found myself wondering if one of these judges might turn out to be prophetic. He said, "They look like a couple who should be married."

These two people:

    a. are strangers posing together

    b. are brother and sister

    c. have been a couple for three months

Answer: c. have been a couple for three months

Accuracy (33.3%)

Women	Men	Total
63.6%	71.9%	67.5%

When I first saw this picture, I thought most of our judges would focus on the way the man is holding the woman. I was wrong. One man did say, "His arms are wrapped around her." But most of our judges were more interested in the expression on these two faces.

It is clear that this picture shows much, much more than just comfort or familiarity. For this reason, only 9 percent of our judges thought these people were brother and sister. Instead, this photograph seemed to bring out the romantic streak in our judges. One man said, "Young love is written all over their faces." A woman said, "She looks possessed," and a man said, "The man looks very 'alive' in this situation—it's an emotional high brought on by a new, active relationship." A woman said, "Their eyes have a dreamy look about them that newly married couples often have." A man also thought this was "the newlywed look," and a woman said, "Bells are ringing."

Several judges seemed to think that the photograph shows even more than simple happiness. One woman commented on their "close physical contact," and another woman said, "They look embarrassed and shy and happy and proud to be with each other." Still another woman said it was clear that "the 'magic' hasn't worn off yet." Perhaps my favorite comment was made by a man who was struck by what seemed like the quiet mystery of their smiles. He said, "They both look like they are posing for Mona Lisa auditions." I cannot imagine a better description.

Summary: Social Intelligence and Recognizing Intimacy

This chapter began by discussing different theories and beliefs about recognizing intimacy. This form of social intelligence consists of the ability to make accurate interpretations about the relationship between two people. Some of the ideas we mentioned were the Hepburn-Finney hypothesis, the front-seat-distance hypothesis, the significance of things as different as newspapers and touching, clothing clues, "lingering looks" and other kinds of eye contact, and matching theory. Social intelligence makes it possible for us to interpret a large number of complex, subtle, and nonverbal clues related to intimacy. We can use this information to try to make accurate guesses about the type of relationship between two people, the "age" of a relationship, or even whether two people are likely to become a couple at all.

The photographs in this chapter capture some of the important qualities of intimacy. From a social intelligence point of view, one of the most significant things about these photographs is simply that they "work"; our judges did much better than guessing or "chance" levels of accuracy. The fact that so many of our judges chose the right answer tells us that *the information is there.* These photographs *do* contain important clues that can be used to answer the questions accompanying the pictures.

We can only learn *what* these clues are, however, by asking our judges. Their comments can tell us how they "read," weigh, and interpret the information in the photographs in order to arrive at the right answers. From the pictures in this chapter, we have learned that there usually is no single clue. Our judges report seeing many different clues in one photograph. The right answer about a given photograph seems to be spread throughout the picture, rather than limited to one small detail. This means that there are several different "routes" to an accurate interpretation.

The explanation for this is that we use our unique social intelligence when we look at a photograph. We tend to see different clues because we have led different lives. The research in this chapter shows that many of these different clues can lead us to the correct interpretation. One strength of this book is that by sharing other people's insights, we can share some aspects of their unique social intelligence.

The comments also reveal some of the judges' ideas about intimacy, love, marriage, and friendship, although this is not the main reason their comments are included. In this chapter, our judges seem to reveal an ambivalence toward love and intimacy.

They are sometimes hopelessly jaded, and sometimes unabashedly romantic. This may be true, of course, of each of us.

The judges discovered a rich treasury of nonverbal clues in the photographs. I would like to summarize some of these clues, but a word of caution is in order. In life, clues are embedded in a complicated mosaic of other details and behaviors. Individual clues probably take on meaning only in light of this contextual information.

As one example, imagine looking at a small detail of a photograph that shows only someone's smile. Our interpretations of this smile could vary enormously. It could be the smile of a bank teller greeting the bank president, the smile of a man watching his three-year-old child at play, the smile of a person laughing with a lover, or even the smile of a defeated athlete as he or she shakes hands with the winner. Without knowing the behavioral context of a single clue like a smile, its real meaning is ambiguous.

I do not believe that any single, specific clue can have exactly the same meaning in all places or at all times. Social intelligence requires the ability to interpret these clues in terms of the context in which they occur. When our judges say that a woman's smile in a photograph is "dreamy," they mean that it looks "dreamy" because of the expression on her face, because of the way the man in the photograph is embracing her, because of the expression on his face, and because of the apparent relationship between the man and woman.

There are, however, several clues that our judges associate with a lack of intimacy. The judges mentioned the distance separating two people. Non-intimates are expected to sit or stand farther apart than intimates. Our judges also expect people married for a short time to stand closer together than people married for a long time. Our judges think that crossed arms indicate discomfort or defensiveness, and therefore a lack of intimacy.

The judges believe that hugging or embracing indicates intimacy, but they also look at facial expressions to see whether people look comfortable with this physical closeness. They look for "natural" eye contact between intimates, and lack of eye contact is interpreted as a sign of unease. Our judges seem to think that non-intimates will smile nervously or giggle when photographed together, while real intimates may not. The judges also expect intimates to be matched on several dimensions, and the older the relationship, the more perfect the match is expected to be.

Some of the judges' most impressive interpretations are more difficult to summarize. They base some of their comments on general impressions that are virtually impossible to explain in words. Each of these impressions probably is based on several, dozens, or perhaps even hundreds of nonverbal clues. Our judges gave us many impressions of this kind: "These two look comfortable," "He looks nervous," "There is no romantic intensity here," and "She looks secure."

Our judges have no difficulty telling us their impressions, even if they cannot explain in words why they have these impressions. As we said earlier, this may be due to the verbal bias of Western culture in general. We do know from the judges' high level of accuracy, however, that these impressions successfully led them to the right answers. Social intelligence apparently requires the ability to read very specific clues as well as the ability to form general impressions.

4 LOVERS AND STRANGERS

The photographs in the last chapter sought to capture natural examples of intimacy or lack of intimacy. These pictures all showed people as our photographer found them. We were very careful not to ask these people to change their behavior in any way.

This chapter is also about intimacy, but its focus is different. Some of the pictures show real couples, but other photographs show "fake couples." We created these fake couples by asking two complete strangers to pose together and to act as if they were a "real couple." Therefore, some photographs show real intimacy, while others show only its imitation. For each question in this chapter, the social intelligence task is to try to guess whether each photograph shows a real couple or a fake couple.

When we decided to take these pictures, we were a little concerned about how the strangers we asked to pose as a couple would respond. After all, it is unusual to pose with a perfect stranger as if you were a loving couple. As it turned out, our fears were groundless. Most people were extremely helpful and obliged us with what seemed like a convincing portrayal of intimacy.

In taking these pictures, we were fascinated by how easily strangers seemed able to pose as a loving couple. I think this shows that there is a social "script" for looking like a loving couple, and that most of us can perform this script quite well. We began to worry that our judges would never be able to tell the difference between real and fake couples. But as we showed the pictures to our judges, we began to notice subtle differences that will be discussed in this chapter.

Some of the people in our fake couples performed so well that they were mistaken for a real couple. In at least one case, the performance was so good that it seemed to convince the performers themselves. As we walked away after taking the picture, the two former strangers were exchanging telephone numbers and agreeing to have lunch together. As far as we know, this is the only case in which one of our fake couples may have become real because of this book.

A word seems in order about the usefulness of fake couples. Since we rarely encounter fake couples in real life, the reader may wonder how studying the simulated intimacy of these couples can contribute to improving our social intelligence. I think that studying simulated intimacy can teach us about the way real intimacy looks. In addition, there are some situations in which we do see fake couples—theatrical drama, movies or television programs, magazine advertisements, and cases of pretended affection in real couples.

Recently, when I met a colleague of mine who teaches theater, I told him about our photographs of fake couples. I asked him whether there are any specific clues that could give a stage couple away. Were actors taught any specific techniques in order to look like a real couple? In general, he said, the answer is no. He felt that what made a couple look convincing was very complicated—how relaxed they looked, how familiar with each other they seemed, and other factors.

He did tell me that when two actors kissed in a performance, he could always tell whether they were seasoned performers or new to the stage. The social intelligence clue? With new or inexperienced actors, the kiss tends to look unnatural because the actors are nervous about pressing their bodies—and particularly their groins—together. As a result, inexperienced actors tend to kiss with their rear ends carefully held back, and the resulting kiss has a "bent-over" look that gives away the fact that it is acted.

Acting, on stage and in the media, is clearly one context in which we all see fake couples. I think simulated intimacy occurs offstage as well. At some point in our lives, who among us has not pretended to like someone better than we really do? Blind dates, junior proms, and flirting behavior would probably disappear if people could not perform more affection than they feel. This kind of performance also explains the surprise that sometimes follows news that a couple has divorced: "The Smiths? I can't believe it. They seemed so happy together."

Some couples, I suppose, have had to pretend intimacy—at least in public—all their lives. In history, monarchs were generally forced to stay married whether happy or not. Henry VIII had six wives, but he is clearly the exception to the rule. A more representative case is that of James I of England. This monarch carefully maintained the public fiction of a satisfying marriage with Anne of Denmark long after the relationship had ended in every important sense. Even today, government officials and other public figures may feel they cannot separate from an unloved spouse. The result, of course, is a public show of affection.

Sometimes, however, the curtain on this performance opens just slightly and we, the audience, get to see backstage. There have been a number of recent kiss-and-tell revelations by acquaintances of presidents and other public figures. These revelations provide a backstage view of the relationship between two members of a public couple. Most of these accounts are in the "demythologizing" genre. They tend to argue that a given public figure's marriage was less loving, or even less monogamous, than its public image. Perhaps the claim that a couple was really *more* loving than their public image would be less newsworthy.

In everyday life, besides seeing simulated intimacy, we may also see precisely the opposite: two people pretending that they are *not* in love. This provides us with a very different opportunity to use our social intelligence. The most obvious example of people concealing their intimacy is probably the case of teen-agers who are trying to keep secret from parents the fact that they are deeply involved. The young lovers may have to work hard to remember not to look at each other or touch each other in a way that could give away the secret of their intimacy.

There are many other examples as well, such as a man and a

woman working in an office and trying to keep their affair secret, or a homosexual couple trying to keep their relationship private. People in these situations may have to try to give a convincing performance of a neutral or nonintimate relationship. This is probably a crushing burden, since it would require two people when they are together to be self-conscious about every gesture, every look, every word, and every touch.

My guess is that these careful acting jobs almost always fail, and that signs of intimacy and passion are likely to "leak" from even the most careful performance. A major reason for this leakage is that social intelligence allows us to pick up subtle clues. We may notice a lingering look, an overlong touch, a loving facial expression, a blush, or "something" in the tone of voice. Real intimacy is, I think, difficult to conceal for long.

I think that unrequited love is still another example of an experience that may lead people to disguise their emotions. One famous case of unrequited love in literature is Edmond Rostand's classic *Cyrano de Bergerac*. Cyrano is desperately in love with the beautiful Roxanne, but because he feels that she could never love him, he never tells her of his love. The secretive nature of his love forces Cyrano to interact with Roxanne in a neutral or platonic manner when in fact he is "consumed" with love for her. The power of this tragic story comes from the fact that the reader knows more than either Cyrano or Roxanne about the true nature of these two people's emotions.

Cyrano probably has many counterparts in real life. Whenever one person feels an attraction or a love for another person without knowing if the feeling is returned, the ingredients for a secret love are present. This unrequited attraction may produce the appearance of a simple friendship, when in fact one of the two people is filled with unspoken love and longing. This person may have to work hard to disguise the true nature of his or her feelings about the other person.

The pictures of fake couples in this chapter may help us to recognize these special cases when people pretend that their emotions and relationships are something other than they are in fact. Pictures of fake intimacy can also teach us about real intimacy.

If we are asked to decide whether a picture shows a real couple or a fake couple, how do we make our decision? I think one way to answer this question is to ask it in a slightly different form: What kinds of things can couples do that two strangers cannot easily imitate? When we decide that something doesn't look "right" in a photograph of a fake couple, this can tell us something about the way we expect a real couple to look. In this way we may learn something about what intimacy is by studying its imitation.

These two people are:

      a. a couple together one year

      b. strangers posing together

Answer: b. strangers posing together

Accuracy (50.0%)

Women	Men	Total
73.0%	71.2%	72.1%

Almost three quarters of our judges correctly guessed that these people are not a real couple. The clues? Many judges commented on the distance between these two people. One woman said that "they seem a little shy of each other," and another woman thought they "look like strangers who don't want to stand near each other to pose for the picture." Several judges thought it was significant that these people were not touching, and one man said, "They are leaning their heads toward each other, but not their bodies." I particularly liked the comment of one man who said, "Physically they are in the picture, but spiritually neither one is."

We tried to create couples who looked believable by matching people in terms of their age and other factors. In this picture, however, we seem to have failed. Many judges said that these two people did not seem matched. One man said, "I can't believe that two people who appear so different have anything in common." Another man said, simply, "She's not his type of woman, and vice versa." The judges thought the woman looks more "formal," "straight," and "studious" than the man. One woman said, "She wouldn't go with a guy who wore a T-shirt like that."

About 28 percent of our judges thought this was a real couple. These judges thought that the shyness in the picture was due to the situation. One woman said, "They look uncomfortable with the camera—they are 'shy' types, but are compatible with each other." Another judge said, "Their shoulders are turned toward one another—they seem to be still growing in their relationship." One woman thought they were matched. She said, "They are both dressed in the way that natural food and health conscious people are." Most judges, however, recognized that this is a fake couple.

These two people are:

    a. a couple together two years

    b. strangers posing together

Answer: a. A couple together two years

Accuracy (50.0%)

Women	Men	Total
69.4%	65.7%	67.5%

Two thirds of our judges guessed correctly that this is a real couple. Matching theory seems to have been involved in our judges' decisions. Both male and female judges said, "They look like they are made for each other." One woman said, "They seem similar in many ways—their clothes and appearance look very similar, possibly adapted from their being together." Another woman said, "They both look happy, and I think they both use the same shampoo." Other judges commented on how close together these people are standing. A man said, "They are leaning toward one another," and a woman said that they seem to have the "same head angle."

Our judges thought that the most impressive thing about this picture was the definite sense, hard to define, that these two people are "together" and happy about it. Several judges commented on the fact that they look "animated" and "comfortable." One woman said, "They are at ease with each other—there is no tension in their faces." A second woman said, "It looks like they enjoy being together," and a third commented, "The expression on their faces is warm and true."

About a third of our judges thought these two people were strangers. One of these judges thought the man's smile was "unnatural," and another said the closeness in this picture looks "rigid." One female judge said of the woman, "Her expression looks like you asked her to pose with this guy." Well, we did. But they are a real couple.

These two people are:

    a. a couple married two years

    b. strangers posing together

Answer: b. strangers posing together

Accuracy (50.0%)

Women	Men	Total
53.3%	48.6%	50.8%

This lively picture made for a very hard question. Our judges did no better than chance, as only half of them guessed that this is a fake couple. The most obvious thing about the photograph is the kiss. If our judges were misled by any single clue, this is it. One man said flatly, "Strangers do not kiss." A woman said, "They look in love, they're both young, and they're kissing—and I mean who kisses strangers?" In case some readers are curious, I should mention that we did not suggest the kiss. It just happened.

Many of our judges tried to interpret what kind of kiss is shown in the picture. Some judges thought the kiss was convincing. One man said the kiss looks "too intimate for strangers," and another man said, "The woman looks like she is loving every minute of acting 'off the wall' in front of the camera—no reservations." One woman said, "They seem to be really enjoying it; I don't think they'd look that happy if they'd never met before."

Other judges disagreed. Half of our judges thought that this kiss is, in their words, a "put-on." A man said, "He kissed her to fool us." One woman said, "He looks crazy enough to kiss a stranger," and another woman said, "This guy looks like he would be a flirt or do something funny for a picture." One man said, "I'd do the same with a chick like that." Some of our judges thought the location of the kiss was significant. One man said, "If they were married, he would not just kiss her cheek," and another man said, "If that was me, I wouldn't be kissing her on the cheek."

Having talked to my colleague in the theater department, I found a clue in the kiss itself. I think that this is the type of kiss that happens between inexperienced actors. The man is leaning over carefully to kiss the woman, and this indicates that they are strangers, not lovers. This may be what one woman meant when she said, "She looks as if she is experiencing a kiss from him for the first time."

Other judges tried to read the woman's face to analyze her reaction. Almost all the judges who did this were women. This may be a matter of identification. One female judge said that the woman looks "surprisingly embarrassed." Many women judges agreed. One said, "She looks too surprised and ebullient about the kiss to look that way after two years of marriage." Two other women tried to imagine themselves in the same situation, and they gave their answer in the form of a question. One said, "Would she laugh if her husband kissed her?" The other asked, "Would you get that hysterical over a kiss on the cheek if it was your husband?" As it turned out, these women were right to be skeptical.

I think there is another important clue in this picture—a clue that none of our judges seemed to see, perhaps because they were blinded by the dazzling kiss. The same thing happened to me, but when I looked at the picture again a few weeks later, I noticed something new. You may already have guessed what it is, but I would like to postpone revealing this clue until after we have looked at more pictures.

These two people are:

    a. a couple married five years

    b. strangers posing together

Answer: b. strangers posing together

Accuracy (50.0%)

Women	Men	Total
81.1%	72.6%	76.5%

Three quarters of our judges guessed that this is a fake couple, and accuracy was even higher (81 percent) among women. Several judges thought the man looked too young. One man said, "The woman looks older than the guy, and he doesn't look old enough to have been married for five years." Some judges thought these two people were an improbable match in other ways. A man said, "She's dressed too formally to be his wife," and a woman said, "They are not wearing clothes fitting the same event, as they would if they were together."

A few judges made attributions about the personalities of these people. These may be projections on the part of our judges, and there is no way of knowing how valid these attributions are. But they are interesting. One woman said, "The people are from two different classes of humans; the woman is more sophisticated than the man." Two other judges expressed this difference in another way. One man said, "The man looks too hip; she looks more serious and settled." The other, a woman, said, "He looks very macho, and she looks very straight, so they are an unlikely match."

The judges who wrongly guessed that this is a married couple were influenced by the smiles in the picture. One woman said they are "enjoying each other's company," and one man even invented additional details, saying, "The woman looks happy, and I think they have some children." The judges who guessed that these people were strangers interpreted these smiles very differently. One judge said the woman seems "rather embarrassed with the situation," and a man said he thought the picture shows "nervous laughter, especially in the woman." Our male judges also speculated about the man's expression. One said, "The woman looks nervous, but the man thinks this is a good way to meet women." Another man said, "I believe he's eyeing the girl next to him, propositioning her for a date, and she's smiling from his request."

Many of our judges didn't think the picture contains any evidence of familiarity. One man said, "This girl is smiling too much, like she doesn't know him." A woman thought they seemed "uncomfortable together" because "they aren't looking at each other." Another woman said, "Closeness seems lacking—I think that two people who were married five years would not hesitate to put their arms around each other."

Finally, one man even had a somewhat male-centered theory about this lack of familiarity. He said, "They are strangers because the man is looking at the woman—if they were married, the man would be looking at the camera and the woman would be looking at the man." An interesting view of relationships!

These two people are:

a. a married couple

b. strangers posing together

Answer: a. a married couple

Accuracy (50.0%)

Women	Men	Total
85.9%	84.5%	85.1%

Almost all of our judges guessed that this is a married couple. Again, matching theory played a part in their decisions. One man said, "They are a good match—they look like they've been married awhile." Many judges seemed to think that these two people are similar in appearance and one man said, "They just look like a matched set." One woman judge noted, "They are wearing the same expression—like they have been molded."

Some judges attributed certain qualities and interests to the people. One woman said, "They look like they enjoy intellectual lifestyles together." Another woman commented, "They both look rugged, with a lot in common." One man made a surprisingly specific guess. He said, "They belong to the Sierra Club." I decided to check this out and was amazed to learn that he was right—these two people are Sierra Club members. How in the world did our judge know this?

Finally, other judges were impressed by the familiarity and closeness visible in this picture. One man said, "She certainly looks too mature and reserved to get that close to a stranger." Another man said, "They appear comfortable—she fits on his shoulder, and this pose would not be spontaneous unless they had been together for some time." A woman said, "They fit together beautifully," and another woman noted, "Instead of standing side by side, they are standing together, sort of connected." One of the better and shorter explanations was given by the man who said, "They're close—they have real smiles."

These two people:

      a. are a couple together five years

      b. are strangers posing together

Answer: b. are strangers posing together

Accuracy (50.0%)

Women	Men	Total
39.0%	46.6%	42.9%

This question is more than hard; it is downright misleading. Only about 43 percent of our judges guessed correctly that these two people are strangers, and this is worse than chance accuracy. Since most of the judges mentioned the position of the woman's arm, I think this is the most misleading part of the picture.

Most judges seemed to think that the position of her arm means that these people must be more than strangers. The problem is that the woman in this photograph is doing a first-rate job of acting. One man said, "Her arm seems to have just the *right* amount of casual intimacy." A woman observed, "They must be a real couple because of the way she is leaning on him with her arm— this is a position strangers would have a hard time getting into." The woman's pose struck the judges as unusual. One man said, "She looks like the boss," and a woman said, "With a stranger, her 'arm-on-top' pose would be threatening or dominating—but with someone she knows well, it is understood and accepted."

The physical contact in this picture makes this a convincing performance of intimacy. Several judges said the two people looked "close," "trusting," and "casual." One woman said, "This picture has an easygoing atmosphere, and very little inhibition." A man said, "The physical contact indicates that these two people are more than strangers."

Not all of our judges were misled in this way; after all, 43 percent did get the right answer. These judges saw this picture very differently. One man said he thought the two people were "hamming it up," and another man noted, "The guy looks too stiff." A woman said, "The pose, while cheerful, is unrelaxed—they are ill at ease."

These judges interpreted the position of the woman's arm in a different light. One woman said, "The way she has her arm on him

seems to be just a friendly gesture—this is not a couple pose."
Another man said, "Her elbow on his shoulder is *not* a gesture of
intimacy between lovers. It is a gesture between strangers or
perhaps friends; they are both wary of each other physically." This
interpretation was seconded by a woman who said, "They look like
they are afraid to touch one another, as strangers would be." I will
save my own comment about this picture until the end of the
chapter.

These two people are:

    a. a married couple

    b. strangers posing together

Answer: a. a married couple

Accuracy (50.0%)

Women	Men	Total
82.0%	63.1%	72.4%

Most of our judges guessed that this is a real couple, and we found a significant sex difference: More women chose the right answer than men. Why did women do much better on this question? I think men seemed to feel that the difference in the smiles of these people was important. One man said, "The woman doesn't seem to be that guy's type—I know that is a poor reason, but it is a feeling I get." Another man said, "The lady is happy to be photographed with the gentleman, while he does not seem to share this feeling."

Women judges, on the other hand, thought these two people were an excellent match. One woman said they "have a settled look" and appear "well suited," and another woman echoed a theory we discussed in the last chapter, "After a certain number of years, people who are married begin to look alike, and these two do." Women interpreted the dissimilarity in the smiles differently. One woman said, "He has an expression of, 'What has she gotten me into now?'" Another woman said, "They look compatible, and they are uncomfortable with the camera but not with each other."

Several judges commented on the distance between the man and woman. One man said, "They seem to share space well, and this indicates a well worked out relationship." One interesting comment was made by the woman who said, "She's relaxed standing close to him, and her age is an important factor—a woman of middle age generally would not feel safe or comfortable that close to a stranger, especially without watching him." Finally, one judge gave a highly personal explanation for his answer. He said, "They are a real couple because they remind me of my parents." An unusual reason, I suppose, but it worked for this judge.

These two people are:

a. a married couple

b. strangers posing together

Answer: b. strangers posing together

Accuracy (50.0%)

Women	Men	Total
62.6%	76.7%	69.8%

Here is a question the men got right. Our male judges were significantly more accurate than our female judges, although both groups did better than chance. Many of our judges thought these two were mismatched in appearance and dress. One woman said, "They don't look compatible—it looks like their lifestyles are vastly different." A man said, "It looks like they just met—why is his shirt off if she's dressed up?" Another man said, "Pardon the lack of seriousness, but I just figured it was not sociable for only one person to be naked!"

Several judges commented on the people's posture. One woman said, "She holds her arms as a barrier; the pose of her head, even though turned toward him, is more of a warning of 'keep your distance' than a reaching out." Another woman observed that "they are close together, but they very carefully are not touching."

Many judges noted that the people in the picture both seemed uneasy. One man said, "The woman seems threatened, and both look like they are unsure." A woman said, "They are having a 'How's the weather?' conversation." A second woman said, "I don't like the way she's looking at him." A third noted, "It looks like there is antagonism between the two people." Other judges agreed. A man said, "They don't look content with each other—if they are married, they don't look happily married." One woman, who guessed that the two people were strangers, hedged her answer by saying, "I suppose they *could* be a married couple having a fight."

Some judges who chose the wrong answer did so because of the same dour view of marriage we encountered in the last chapter. These judges guessed that the two people were married *because* they seemed miserable. One man said, "The eyes lack the dazzle that seems to occur when strangers meet." Another man said, "The turmoil of marriage seems evident." A woman said, "Strangers would smile at the camera—this looks like a married couple having a fight." Perhaps the shortest and most bitter explanation was given by the man who said simply, "Strangers don't bitch at each other." Most of our judges, however, were able to tell that this picture does not show soured intimacy but only its complete absence.

These two people:

    a. say they are in love

    b. are strangers posing together

Answer: a. say they are in love

Accuracy (50.0%)

Women	Men	Total
50.9%	37.2%	44.6%

    This is another difficult question. Only about 45 percent of our judges recognized that these two people are not strangers. The woman is seated on the man's lap, and this fact seemed to influence many judges. One woman said, "She looks carefree and happy, and her sitting on his lap seems very natural." A man said, "She seems to be sitting on his lap, and if they were strangers, I think their expressions would be different." A woman said simply, "Strangers don't sit on each other's lap." Other judges disagreed about this clue. One woman said, "I would look away like the girl if I had to sit on a stranger's lap."

    Most judges looked for clues that could show how the man and woman were reacting to this physical closeness. Many judges thought they detected signs of discomfort in one or both of the people. One man said, "She looks embarrassed to be seen with this guy." A woman said, "The woman looks like she's holding tightly on to her purse—perhaps mistrustful of strangers?" A man said, "She doesn't seem to be serious enough for love!" Commenting about the man, one woman said, "The man doesn't look comfortable next to her—his eyes don't reveal a closeness or fondness for her." Another woman said, "They are turning away from each other." One of the most intriguing comments was made by the woman who said, "She is sitting on his lap, but there is no 'mental touching.' " These clues led one man to say, "They may very well be in love, but I doubt if they are in love with each other."

    These comments are interesting, but this picture does show a real couple. Perhaps these judges were picking up misleading clues, or perhaps they were detecting a genuine lack of affection in this relationship. Some judges did see intimacy in this photograph. One woman said, "It looks like they just told you they were in love because they both look a bit flustered." A man said, "He's showing affection for her," and a woman said, "He looks as if he wants to show her off." Another judge said, "They look like a pair of compatible free spirits."

Some of the judges who chose the right answer seemed to hedge their answers. One woman said, "They don't really look in love—but they seem like they know each other." Finally, one man noticed the fact that the wording of the answer is that these two people "say they are in love." He said, "This is excellent syntax because these two have a relationship, but it's on the way down. But they still maintain that they are in love." It would be interesting to follow up this couple to see if the pessimistic predictions of many of our judges come true.

Summary: Lovers, Strangers, and the Waxy Hand Effect

The photographs and questions in this chapter deal with a special aspect of intimacy: the difference between a genuine relationship and its imitation. In the case of a few photographs, it was hard for our judges to tell whether or not they were seeing a real couple. In general, however, our judges did surprisingly well, particularly since I thought we had created some very convincing fake couples.

This ability to recognize genuine intimacy is very impressive. I think it is an important finding, demonstrating that intimacy is extremely hard to imitate. Even if two people are trying to act like a loving and intimate couple, the performance is unlikely to succeed unless a genuine relationship exists between them.

One reason for this is familiarity. When we have an intimate and long-standing relationship with someone, our movements have a smooth, almost synchronized quality. In an intimate relationship, one rarely sees awkward movements, stiff-looking embraces, or embarrassment. Even though our fake couples were trying to look authentic, they must have looked uncomfortable in some of these ways.

Earlier in this chapter, in connection with the splendid kiss in the picture on page 71, I mentioned that there was an important clue to intimacy in this picture that none of our judges seemed to see. I would like to return to this clue now.

In general, I think social intelligence rarely rests on a *single* clue. When we interpret a photograph or behavior in real life, we may have dozens or even hundreds of clues available. It is the way these clues fit together that strikes our social intelligence as important or significant—for example, physical closeness *combined* with relaxed facial expressions. Social intelligence generally requires us to understand these combinations of clues.

In the case of our fake couples, however, I think we may have discovered a single, significant clue that is impressively consistent and revealing. What is this clue? I think that one of the most important clues to people's relationships can be found in their hands and hand positions. Even when people are trying to act like a couple, they seem to be betrayed by their hands. The hands in the photographs of our fake couples look tense, formal, prudent, unconvincing and carefully asexual.

I call this the "waxy hand effect," and I think it provides an excellent clue for recognizing intimacy. The explanation of the waxy hand effect is that it seems to be relatively easy to perform intimacy in one's face; we can all fake a friendly, happy, or affectionate facial expression. Hands are more difficult to control, particularly since our fake couples are frequently pictured arm in arm. They are touching and holding each other in a way that non-intimates rarely do. Our society has a strong prohibition or "taboo" against touching strangers in this way, and the tension caused by this taboo is evidenced in the waxy hand effect.

Hands, therefore, may be a kind of "lie detector" against which the rest of the performance can be judged. If the hands somehow do not look "right," we are probably looking at feigned intimacy rather than the real thing. In two of our photographs, we have a good opportunity to study the waxy hand effect; we photographed the same man as part of a fake and a real couple. These photographs were taken before we discovered the waxy hand effect, and they do not show as much of the hands and arms as we would like. Opposite are both photographs.

Since you saw the real couple in the last chapter (page 39), you already know that the first couple is a fake, while the second couple is real. We showed these two photographs to two different groups of judges. Our judges did well on recognizing the real couple (78.6 percent correctly identified the real couple), but many judges were fooled by the fake couple. Only 44.8 percent of our judges could tell that the first couple was a fake.

In some ways, you can see why the judges were fooled. Since the two pictures were shown to different groups of judges, the judges could not compare the two pictures. When you see both pictures together, the first seems wooden or artificial in comparison with the second. Our judges may also have been fooled by the first picture because it contains some clues to intimacy such as eye contact and smiles.

If our judges had known about the waxy hand effect, I do not think they would have been fooled by the first picture. Compare the man's hand and arm in the two pictures. In the second picture (the real couple), the man's arm forms a relaxed, natural curve around the woman. He seems to feel that their relationship entitles him to hold her in this way.

In the first picture (the fake couple), we see an excellent illustration of the waxy hand effect. The man's hand is perched in a carefully nonsexual way upon the woman's shoulder. His hand almost looks like an epaulet on a uniform, and it is not even certain from the photograph that the man's fingers are actually touching the woman's jacket. Some of our judges picked this up. They called the postures "stiff," and one judge said, "The placement of the man's arm looks too precarious." My favorite comment eloquently describes the basic idea behind the waxy hand effect. This judge, a woman, said, "The warmth of the man's smile is excessive in comparison with the rest of his body language. His arm is stiff."

Let's return to the photograph on page 71. When I first saw this picture, all I saw was the kiss. It seems like a conclusive clue, and along with about half of our judges, I probably would have guessed (wrongly) that these two were married. Now we will make a closer inspection of the man's hand. Opposite is the picture you saw earlier, as well as an additional picture taken seconds before the

kiss. These photographs offer a classic illustration of the waxy hand effect. The man is trying to demonstrate intimacy, and he seems to be doing a convincing job. In both photographs, however, he is carefully holding the woman at the top of her shoulder near the back of her neck—a safe, nonsexual area. His hand is gingerly and, I think, unnaturally positioned. Most of his hand is placed on the woman's back. Real intimacy probably would make the man feel he had the "right" to hold the woman in a more sexual way, with a hand on her side or around her waist. Since he is only posing, he holds his hand in a controlled and sexually neutral position.

Other fake couples we photographed offer additional evidence of the waxy hand effect. The picture on page 77—the one with the woman leaning her arm on the man—is another example. The woman's arm looks convincing, but actually this pose allows her to avoid touching the man with her hand. Very briefly, and almost without comment, I would like to show some other fake couples we photographed. If the following photographs are any guide, the discovery of the waxy hand effect may be significant. For each of the following photographs, no more than one or two judges (out of two hundred) commented on the unconvincing look of the people's hands. I think knowing about the waxy hand effect would have led more judges to the right answer.

In response to this photograph, one woman judge said, "The man's hand doesn't know what to do—it isn't relaxed." A man said, "His embrace is high on her shoulder, close to the neck."

In this picture of a fake couple, the man's fist is clenched. His fingers could not be in a less intimate position. Some of our judges actually misperceived this picture; one man said, "He's grasping her."

In these two photographs, the woman places an arm around the man. You have seen the people in one of these fake couples before, on page 37. After the people had posed naturally for that picture, we asked them to pretend to be a couple, and the results are shown here. In both pictures, I think the woman's hand looks like a dead fish. The hand lies limply on the man's shoulder, and it is clearly there tentatively. There is no sign that the woman is really holding the man. One woman judge said of the first picture, "Their arms have a noncommittal flare." About the second picture, another woman said, "Her hand doesn't seem to *feel* his shoulder."

I suppose this picture shows the ultimate extension of the waxy hand effect. The man solves the problem of what to do with his hand by keeping it as far from the woman's body as possible. Some of our judges cleverly picked up this clue. One woman said, "He doesn't dare to put his arm around her even though the photographer asked him to."

I think the waxy hand effect is an excellent clue (and in some cases the only clue) as to whether two people are really a couple. Our photographs of fake couples show that even though most people can "face" posing like a real couple, they may not be able to "handle" it convincingly.

5 KINSHIP CLUES

Most of us are involved in some form of kinship system. All of us have been children, some of us are parents, and many of us also are involved in a network of brothers, sisters, cousins, aunts, uncles, grandparents, grandchildren, and in-laws. These are some of the most enduring relationships in our society. Even if these relationships are occasionally strained, there is no legal mechanism for divorcing our kinfolk.

As in the case of intimate relationships, kinship interactions tend to follow a certain social script. In families in our society, for example, it is the father or mother—and almost never the child—who sits at the end of a dinner table. This can be somewhat complicated in multi-generational families because there may be several fathers and mothers present. An example of this is a large family gathering at Thanksgiving. I think that the usual American solution to this problem is for the grandparents to relinquish the table's ends to the parents. This may reflect the reduced position of older people in our society compared to some other societies.

Kinship scripts contain informal rules, rights, and responsibilities that determine the way we "ought" to behave toward our kinfolk. As one example, it seems to me that a key script for being a parent involves giving advice. This is an easy habit to acquire, and I am sometimes amazed at how often I give advice to my four-year-old son: "Watch out for that stick"; "Don't touch the heater"; "Be nice to the kitty."

This advice-giving kinship script is much easier to acquire than it is to shed. Parents may continue to give unsolicited advice to their children when the children are grown or even middle aged. I once overheard a conversation between a man and his thirty-year-old son. In less than three minutes and with no prompting from his son, the father managed to give advice on five separate topics. I doubt that this man would have inflicted this blizzard of suggestions on a friend, co-worker, or spouse.

The license to advise may be a unique feature of parent-child relationships. I think this is a useful item of social intelligence. Whenever I overhear one-sided advice in a conversation between an older person and a younger person, I tend to assume that they are parent and child. There is also a physical version of the advice-giving script. Particularly when their children are young, parents will often grab them, adjust their clothing, button an unbuttoned shirt, or smooth tousled hair. Parental touching also seems to persist when the child has grown up. One woman I know told me that her mother unconsciously continues to adjust her hairstyle, although the daughter is thirty-four years old.

It has always seemed to me that this particular kinship script plays a key role in conflict between the generations. Older children may start to resent the same behavior that was more readily accepted when they were younger. The parent script contains highly symbolic acts such as giving unsolicited advice, which reminds a grown child of both the parent's authority and the child's former dependence. In any interaction, the father and mother may be performing, perhaps unconsciously or out of habit, the parent script, but the grown son or daughter may be concerned about being independent and may refuse to play the child script. This conflict of scripts may be one reason why dialogue across the generations tends to be more sensitive and complicated than other interactions.

Kinship scripts are an important source of data for our social intelligence. If we are sensitive to the advice-giving script, it may help us to recognize a parent-child interaction. I have a friend who receives frequent phone calls from his parents. Although normally a very congenial person, he often becomes very testy during these phone calls. The tone of his voice is impatient, exasperated, and argumentative. Since this is so unlike his usual behavior, his manner is a perfectly reliable social intelligence clue. I can always tell when his parents are on the phone. I also wonder about his parents' perceptions of their son, since they must see a very different person than I see.

Robin Akert and I made a videotape of a phone call between a woman college student and her mother. We explained to the student that we were interested in parent-child interactions, and we obtained her permission to make a videotape while she telephoned her mother. Although we could not hear anything the mother said, it must have been a classic version of the advice-giving script. My guess is that the mother and daughter were having a very testy exchange. The student said very little during the call. During one thirty-nine-second segment (which is a long time in a conversation), the student said only the following twelve words: "I understand that, you know, um . . . I'm not, you know, I'll . . . that's fine."

We showed this videotape to over a thousand college students and asked them to guess whether the woman was talking to her mother, her father, or a friend. These judges did quite well. Since our question had three possible answers, only a third of our judges should have chosen the right answer by random guessing. Fully 55 percent, however, knew that the woman was talking to her mother. Clearly, there are some kinship clues in this videotape.

It seems to me that parent-child relationships follow a developmental sequence of several stages. Certain aspects of the kinship script, like advice giving, may be found in all of these stages. In other ways, the kinship script changes as the child grows and the parent-child relationship focuses on different issues and themes. These changes in the kinship script are a useful source of social intelligence, since we can expect to see different kinship clues in each developmental stage.

It is almost as if parents and children are following the script of a play in several acts. Each act of this play is dominated by a specific set of concerns, and these concerns can provide valuable clues. While dining in a restaurant recently, I noticed a man sit down at the next table. He very carefully moved all the loose objects on one side of the table—water glasses, silverware, napkins, and a flower vase—into the exact center of the table. He must have seemed deranged to most of the restaurant's patrons. Having just passed through a certain parent-child stage, however, I guessed that this man was meeting an 18-month-old for lunch. A few minutes later, the mother and child arrived, and the child was seated at the side of the table her father had defensively cleared for her.

From the child's point of view, it seems to me that the major theme of each stage of the parent-child relationship might be something like the following: total dependence (from when the child is born to two and one-half years old); language and struggle (two and one-half to four); growing competence and independence (five to ten); embarrassment over parents (eleven to seventeen); acceptance of parents (eighteen to twenty-five); partial or full identification with parents (after age twenty-five and particularly when the child becomes a parent); and finally, perhaps even role reversal (the middle-aged child assists or gives advice to an aging parent). These changes in the parent-child relationship are what Mark Twain had in mind when he said, "When I was a boy of fourteen, my father was so ignorant I could hardly stand to have the old man around. But when I got to be twenty-one, I was astonished at how much he had learned in seven years."

Parent-child interactions differ in each stage of this sequence. A number of psychologists have recently studied the way a parent interacts with a very young child. This is sometimes called research on the "caregiver" to avoid the assumption that mothers will be taking care of children, while fathers will not. Recent research has focused on the caregiver's verbal and nonverbal behavior. For example, researchers are now taking a closer look at "baby talk." It has been discovered that baby talk seems to be an excellent way to teach language. It is as if parents "know" unconsciously how to simplify their speech in just the right ways.

As just a single example, when parents speak baby talk to their infants they are apt to avoid the complication of pronouns. A parent may say, "Oh, Mommy dropped the ball—Mommy will get the ball," instead of, "Oh, Mommy dropped the ball—I'll get it." This facilitates language learning by allowing the child to associate a single name with each person or object. As the child grows older, the difference between nouns and pronouns becomes clear. But baby talk appears to be an extremely efficient way of introducing a child to language.

Some aspects of the way parents interact with their children are absolutely remarkable. When a parent interacts with an infant, there is much more than baby talk involved. The parent is likely to talk to the infant with the child held just inches away from the adult's face. The parent's face will light up with greatly exaggerated expressions—arched eyebrows, pursed lips, and wide-open eyes. The parent will speak in an unnaturally high-pitched voice and will probably make sounds (such as clucking and bubbling) that have nothing to do with real words. We tend to take this behavior pretty much for granted, but the parent's behavior is clearly remarkable. The next time you see a parent playing with an infant, try to imagine the parent behaving this way toward another adult. It would be nothing less than bizarre.

Robin Akert and I once videotaped two women playing with a seven-month-old child. Opposite are a photograph taken from this videotape and a transcript of about thirty seconds of the actual interaction.

WOMAN ON RIGHT: Oh, who's got you? . . . Who's got you? Huh?
[Baby makes noise.]
Oh, there are more flowers on that side . . . more flowers on
that side.
WOMAN ON LEFT: Ahh . . . Oh, look at that boy.
[Baby makes noise.]
WOMAN ON RIGHT: Whatcha doin'? . . . What are you doing?
Huh?
WOMAN ON LEFT: Hello . . . Look at that smile.
WOMAN ON RIGHT: Ah, can you hold that big smile? That's a boy.
WOMAN ON LEFT: Who are you laughing at?
WOMAN ON RIGHT: Where's your big smile? . . . Come here, ahh,
umm.
WOMAN ON LEFT: Zachary, she's eating you!
WOMAN ON RIGHT: Umm.

Is one of these two women the child's mother? We asked a large number of judges to try to guess if the woman on the left is the mother, if the woman on the right is the mother, or if neither woman is the child's mother. When we showed only this transcript (no picture or videotape) to one group of judges, only 50 percent of these judges guessed the right answer. The correct answer is that the woman on the right is the child's mother. Judges who were shown the videotape did much better—64 percent of these judges correctly guessed who the mother was.

I think this is further evidence that social intelligence is not just a matter of language. The judges who saw the videotape were more accurate because they had more than words to go on. They could see what the two women looked like, how they behaved, how they touched the child, and how their voices sounded. As one example, several judges who saw the videotape said that the woman on the left acted as if she had not held the baby before. One judge said, "She is holding the baby as if he were made of porcelain." By contrast, another judge said, "The woman on the right isn't afraid to touch the child."

So far, we have discussed only interaction clues—how people in a kinship relationship behave toward each other. I think there are other clues to kinship, and some of these are the kinds of visual clues that can be detected even from photographs.

Visual details sometimes offer the most striking clues to kinship, and most of us do expect children to resemble their parents. I think there are actually two kinds of kinship similarity. The first and most obvious is *physical inheritance.* Physical resemblance is the product of genetic factors, and there are many families in which this resemblance is pronounced. I know one woman who looks uncannily like her four sisters. For this reason, I was not surprised when this woman gave birth to a baby who looked like a clone of the mother.

Physical resemblance is also partly in the eye of the beholder. I know a family in which there are two boys the same age; one is adopted, and the other is the biological child of the parents. The parents tell me that many people have said to them, "I can tell this one is 'yours' because he looks *just* like you—the other boy is obviously adopted." The interesting thing is that the parents have kept track of these guesses, and they tell me that only 50 percent of the people are right; people are no more accurate than chance. Even the social worker who placed the adopted boy with the family guessed wrong!

The beholder's eye is an important factor in recognizing kinship. When we see a child together with one parent, we may tend to see more similarity between them than actually exists. This is because it is easier to see similarities between two people once we know they are related. All my friends tell me that my sons look just like me, while their mother's friends say they are a mirror image of her.

Physical inheritance is only one type of kinship similarity. There is also *social inheritance*. Children tend to resemble their parents because children tend to participate in the parents' values and lifestyles. For example, I know a psychologist who is a very flamboyant dresser. She tends to wear enormous hoop earrings and brightly embroidered dresses. The net effect is a sort of "gypsy" look. I once attended a party where I met a young woman who was dressed just like my acquaintance the psychologist. The similarity struck me as a remarkable coincidence until I discovered that the young woman is the psychologist's daughter! In this case the mother's style has been "inherited" along with her genes.

Even basic physical traits can reflect our social inheritance. There are often consistent styles in the way family members eat. Consequently, it is not unusual to find fat families, and families in which all the members tend to be slim. Eating habits, like styles of dress, are an important part of our social inheritance.

All of these factors—parent-child scripts, physical inheritance, and social inheritance—provide clues we can use to recognize a bond of kinship. In everyday life, we are sometimes given a chance to test our ability to read kinship clues. As one example, take the case of fast-food restaurants. The next time you enter one of these establishments, you can construct a simple kinship test. Choose three adults who are at the counter waiting to be served. Then look around the booths or seats in the room and see if you can guess which family belongs with each of the adults at the counter. This is a perfect social intelligence item, since you can check your guesses when the adults sit down with their families.

The kinship photographs in this chapter contain some of the clues we might see in everyday life. Photographs can capture visual aspects of a person's physical inheritance and social inheritance. They can also capture a single instant or "slice" of parent-child interaction. This is less information than we have to go on in real life, but as the following photographs show, it can still be enough.

Which of these two men is the father of the little boy?

    a. the man on the left

    b. the man on the right

Answer: b. the man on the right

Accuracy (50.0%)

Women	Men	Total
70.0%	**71.4%**	**70.7%**

Our judges did quite well on this question—seven out of ten guessed correctly that the boy's father is the man on the right. I have mentioned two types of kinship clues: *interaction* clues and the *visual* clues of our physical and social inheritance. When they looked at this picture, our judges thought they detected both types of kinship clues.

Two of the more striking interaction clues are the direction of the father's gaze and the expression on his face. One judge said, "The man on the right looks at the boy; the man on the left looks at the camera." A woman judge said, "The man on the right seems more interested in the little boy—he seems to be getting pleasure from the little boy's reactions rather than merely posing for the picture." Some judges read a number of different kinship behaviors in the father's face. One man said, "He seems to be interested in how the kid will look in the picture, whereas the man on the left is more concerned with how he himself looks." Another man said, "The father is trying to make his son smile."

Other judges were struck by the paternal facial expression of the man on the right. Judges described this expression as "protective," "possessive," "proud," and "admiring." After looking at the picture, one man said, "I have a feeling that the man on the right is looking after the boy." One woman explained her choice of the man on the right by saying simply, "Because of the loving way he is looking at the boy."

Other judges cited visual clues. One man said the man on the right "looks more like the stereotype father." Other judges said this man looks "more conservative," "more settled," and "more of a father figure." One woman said, "He's clean-shaven (more of a father type)."

Some judges also thought they detected a resemblance between the boy and the man on the right. One social similarity clue was noticed only by women judges. This clue is clothing. A number of women said the boy's clothes—a denim shirt over a T-shirt—are a junior version of what the man on the right is wearing. One woman said, "These two look like their clothes were selected by the same woman."

Finally, there is the clue of physical inheritance. One woman said that the boy and the man on the right "have the same eyes and mouth." This picture, however, also demonstrates the power of the beholder's eye. Other judges thought that the boy looks just like the man on the left. These judges wrongly chose the man on the left as the boy's father because of "similarities" in their hair color and length, and features. In this picture, at least, anatomical clues were unreliable. The judges who correctly "detected" the father in this picture focused on interaction clues rather than physical resemblance.

Which one of these two women is the mother of these children?

     a. the woman on the left

     b. the woman on the right

Answer: a. the woman on the left

   Accuracy (50.0%)

Women	Men	Total
82.0%	80.0%	81.0%

This question is an easy one, and almost all of our judges guessed correctly that the woman on the left is the mother of the two boys. The most important clues seem to be the interaction clues. Judges who tried to see a physical resemblance between mother and children were led astray. Several of these judges thought that the kids' facial features matched those of the woman on the right, and these judges wrongly identified her as the mother.

Interaction clues were more reliable. Many of our judges were struck by the sharp contrast in the body positions of the two boys. One man said, "The child on the left is cuddled up to his mother, but the child on the right seems to have an expression on his face like, 'Hurry up and take the picture so this woman can let go of me.' " A woman judge agreed, saying, "The kid on the left is leaning in lovingly, while the other kid is stiff and cold to the lady next to him." One man who identified the woman on the left as the mother said, "If I'm wrong, the kid on the left is a great actor!"

Other judges noticed additional clues. A man said, "The boy on the left has his finger in his mouth—a behavior that would be very unlikely if he felt any inhibitions." Several judges commented on the facial expression of the woman on the left. These judges said she appeared to be "comforting the child," and one man said, "She is looking admiringly at the child."

Finally, one judge was struck by a small but very interesting detail: the difference in the two women's hands. This man said, "The woman on the right just barely touches the boy with a closed hand—she doesn't *really* hold him." Looking at the picture, I must say that her hand does look like the waxy hand effect described in the last chapter. Once again, the hands seem to be a reliable index as to whether or not a person is comfortable.

Man 1   Man 2

This young man is the son of one of these two men. Who is the father?

    a. Man 1

    b. Man 2

Answer: b. Man 2

    Accuracy (50.0%)

Women	Men	Total
66.7%	62.0%	64.3%

In this question, there are no interaction clues. The three men are shown in separate pictures, so our judges were forced to base their answers only on appearance. The absence of interaction clues may be one reason that this question was relatively difficult.

Even without any interaction clues, most of our judges managed to identify the man's father. Some of our judges could not explain in detail the reasons for their choice, saying only, "They look more alike." Several judges commented on the build of the men. One woman said, "It could be either man, but I chose Man 2 because I assume father and son would both be slim."

Other judges thought they detected some physical resemblance between the young man and Man 2. Some judges cited specific anatomical details like "thin lips," "almond-shaped eyes," and "narrower bone structure in the cheeks and above the eyebrows." Some judges commented that these two men have "broad, openmouthed smiles," and "their eyes close when they smile." I agree that physical similarities of this kind can be seen in these pictures, and the fact that 64 percent of the judges chose the right answer supports this.

As with other pictures, however, some judges thought they saw similarities in the other direction. These judges wrongly chose Man 1 as the father. One woman said that the young man and Man 1 have "similar facial lines." Another woman said she saw in both these men "the same deep sense of mirth."

There is also the matter of the beards. Some judges wrongly picked Man 1 as the father because both he and the young man have beards. However, I was fascinated to see that most of our judges made the opposite interpretation. One man said the young man's beard was probably "a sign of independence," and another thought it indicated "rebellion." A third man said, "It has been my

experience that a bearded son has a father without a beard."
Finally, a woman judge also agreed, saying, "A straight-looking
father many times has a long-haired son, although the son will
share the father's mental characteristics." I don't know if these
judges are right about the link between bearded sons and unbeard-
ed fathers, but they did pick the right man as the father.

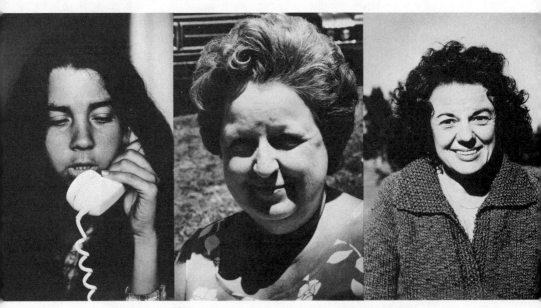

Woman 1   Woman 2

**The woman on the telephone is the daughter of one of these
two women. Who is the mother?**

    a. Woman 1

    b. Woman 2

Answer: b. Woman 2

Accuracy (50.0%)

Women	Men	Total
73.0%	71.2%	72.1%

Even without any interaction clues to guide them, our judges did better on this item than on the previous question. Most judges based their answers on physical resemblance. Judges said they thought that the young woman and Woman 2 have similar "hair color and texture," "nose shapes," "foreheads," and "expressions." One woman said, "They're about the right age, and both mother and daughter look vivacious."

Several judges commented that the young woman and Woman 2 seemed similar in personality, although it is not clear how our judges could read personality traits from photographs. One woman said these two women seem "more open," and a man said they both look "intense."

Judges who wrongly chose Woman 1 also thought they saw personality similarities. One man said the young woman and Woman 1 both look "serious," and another man said, "They both look angry—maybe angry parents raise angry kids." Finally, a woman who wrongly chose Woman 1 said, "The daughter looks strong-willed, and Woman 1 looks like your basic oppressed housewife—it just fits."

There was room for disagreement about personality traits even among judges who chose the right answer. One judge said Woman 2 and her daughter look like "free and easygoing people," and another judge said they both "appear slightly anxious"! Despite this kind of disagreement, most of our judges had little trouble matching Woman 2 and her daughter.

This woman is:

        a. waking her husband from a nap

        b. watching an arm-wrestling match

        c. playing with her baby daughter

Answer: c. playing with her baby daughter

Accuracy (33.3%)

Women	Men	Total
89.9%	76.8%	83.3%

As this second photograph reveals, the woman is playing with her daughter. This was a very readable picture for our judges. Although only a third of our judges could be expected to get the right answer by chance alone, more than 80 percent guessed that the woman is with her daughter. For some reason, our women judges did significantly better than our men judges on this question—about nine women in ten chose the right answer.

How did our judges do so well? Many judges said that this woman's expression is "loving," and most judges felt positive that her face shows love for a child rather than an adult. Although I do not really understand how our judges knew this, it led them to decide that the woman was not waking her husband from a nap—only about 13 percent of our judges chose this answer.

Many judges said the picture shows "maternal love." One man said the woman must be "looking at something innocent," and another man said her face shows "love which could only be for a child." A third man called her expression "that love-a-baby look." Women judges tended to use more specific descriptions. They said the woman's face shows "contentment," "pleasure," "pride," "tenderness," "softness," "adoration," and even "awe." Women judges also thought that the woman's face shows that she is looking at someone she "takes care of" and "looks after."

Only about 17 percent of our judges chose the wrong answer on this question. One judge thought the woman looked too young to have a husband or a child. A woman judge thought the woman in the picture is "looking sexy," and another thought her face shows "the gentle look of love for her husband." One man thought the woman's smile indicated that "her husband has a goofy face." For the overwhelming majority of our judges, however, this picture was an easily read portrait of maternal affection.

The man on the right in each picture is the father of:

    a. the little girl

    b. the little boy

Answer: a. the little girl

Accuracy (50.0%)

Women	Men	Total
62.9%	**64.2%**	**63.5%**

Although this was a fairly difficult question, most of our judges guessed correctly that the little girl is the man's child. Our judges based their answers on various interaction clues. Many people thought the man looks more relaxed when he is holding the girl on his lap. One man said, "With the boy, he stares too intently at the camera, but with the girl his expression lightens up."

Several judges thought they saw an important difference in the way the man holds the children. One judge said, "He is holding the girl much closer to himself," and another judge felt that the man was "just holding the boy, but clasping the girl tightly." Judges who chose the right answer also thought the little girl looked more at ease than the little boy. One woman said the girl seemed more "outgoing toward the photographer," and a man said, "There is a sense of closeness and happiness about the girl, while the boy seems distant and aloof." I particularly liked the comment of the man who said simply, "She likes him."

Judges who incorrectly chose the boy had a variety of reasons for their choice. One judge thought the boy's smile indicated relaxation, although this smile strikes me as forced. One woman based her answer on appearance and said, "The boy looks just like his daddy." This is another case where the resemblance may be mainly in the beholder's eye. A second woman said, "The boy looks like he could sit there for a long time, but the girl seems to be struggling to get away." This is an interesting error, because it is the kind of mistake that is only possible with a photograph. If this judge had seen these people being photographed, she would have known immediately that the little girl was animated or happy and not struggling.

Is this woman the boy's mother?

    a. yes

    b. no

Answer: b. no

Accuracy (50.0%)

Women	Men	Total
70.4%	61.2%	65.8%

About two thirds of our judges recognized that this picture does not show a mother and her child. Once again, we have the problem of the beholder's eye, and appearance clues seemed to be of little use. One man said, "They're certainly look-alikes," but another man said, "He doesn't look at all like her." The most important clues were interaction clues. Many judges had the feeling that this picture just did not look "right." As one woman said, "Although she's got her arm around him, it doesn't look as secure or close as I feel it would be if he were her son." Similarly, a man said, "Although they are in close physical proximity, their closeness doesn't convey familiarity."

Several judges tried to interpret the child's reaction to the woman. One woman said, "The boy looks somewhat reluctant to be sitting on the woman's lap—he doesn't seem quite at home." Judges who thought that the woman was the child's mother thought the bottle was significant. One woman said, "He feels comfortable drinking in her arms." Another judge said the child's position was just playful "squirming" on his mother's lap. Most judges, however, read these clues as signs of discomfort. One man said, "The woman appears ill at ease—look at the way she's adjusting her glasses." One woman said, "She looks like she doesn't know what to do with him—she could be an aunt, maybe, but she's not the mother."

Two of our judges offered brief but telling comments. One said, "There's not much warmth here," and the other said, "There is nothing attaching one to the other."

These two people are:

        a. strangers posing together

        b. father and son

        c. salesmen in a car dealership

Answer: b. father and son

Accuracy (33.3%)

Women	Men	Total
73.0%	74.0%	73.5%

Most of our judges guessed correctly that these two men are father and son. One woman said, "They seem as though they've known each other awhile—they are relaxed and unreserved." Another woman said, "There is a 'personalness' to the picture because they share something together." Our judges seemed particularly struck by the look on the son's face. One woman said, "They're father and son because of the way the younger guy is looking at the older one." Another judge, a man, said, "The son looks at the father with respect."

Several judges also said they saw great similarities in the men's appearance. Judges commented on the "same moustache," "look-alike eyebrows," "carbon copy clothes," and even "the exact same wave in their hair." Once again, our judges were not unanimous on the question of appearance. One judge who thought the two men were salesmen said, "They seem to know each other, but they are very different, as if they were brought together only by business." Three quarters of our judges, however, were sure they detected the unmistakable signs of an important relationship in these two photographs. One of these judges, a woman, said, "They love each other—there's a kinship between them."

The kinship photographs we have looked at so far have all been fairly decodable. Although some of these questions have been relatively difficult, our judges performed above chance levels of accuracy on each question. The final two questions in this chapter are much more difficult. On one of them, our judges did much worse than chance. I have included these pictures to show that the clues to kinship are sometimes difficult to read. Here is the first of these two questions.

These two women are:

    a. a mother and daughter having a picnic

    b. clerks in a stationery store who are on their lunch break

    c. strangers who agreed to be photographed together

Answer: a. a mother and daughter having a picnic

Accuracy (33.3%)

Women	Men	Total
43.0%	45.9%	44.4%

Overall, our judges did barely better than chance on this item. I think one reason they did not do well is the wording of the question. Judges had two possible reasons for *not* choosing the right answer—because they thought the women are not mother and daughter, or because they thought the photograph does not look like a picnic scene. This second factor clearly influenced some judges. One man said, "They're not having a picnic because they're not in a terrific setting for a picnic." Similarly, one woman said, "On picnics, people relax instead of wearing buttoned-up coats."

Despite the poor wording of the question, about 44 percent of our judges decided correctly that the two women in the picture are mother and daughter. One man commented that the two women are "leaning in slightly to indicate that they know each other." A woman said that they show a "comfortable manner of sitting," and another woman thought that they share the "same posture." Some of our judges showed a keen attention to details in this photograph. One woman decided that this is a picnic scene because "There is a bread wrapper at the bottom of the picture and a half-eaten apple."

Judges disagreed about whether the women resemble each other. Some of our judges thought these women look very much alike. One man said, "It looks like they bought their jackets at the same place," and another man commented on their "similar lips, facial features, and hair parting." Other judges said they saw absolutely no resemblance between the women!

Several judges incorrectly concluded that these women were not mother and daughter because they are seated relatively far apart. I think this distance is just the normal "picnic distance," and there is some picnic food placed between the women.

Picture 1

Picture 2

In one of these two pictures, the man with the beard is talking with his son. Which picture shows the son?

        a. Picture 1

        b. Picture 2

Answer: a. Picture 1

Accuracy (50.0%)

Women	Men	Total
35.0%	33.0%	34.0%

These pictures are downright misleading, and our judges did worse than chance. The father and son are shown standing in front of the flowering tree in Picture 1. One of the reasons for our judges' poor performance again appears to be the problem of the beholder's eye. A great many judges decided that the men in Picture 2 were father and son because of their "similar noses." For example, one man said, "The slope of the noses of the men in Picture 2 seems closer." Some judges, however, chose Picture 1 on the basis of appearance. One woman chose this picture because, "The bone structure of the head and face are more similar."

Our judges were also influenced by the smiles of the men in Picture 2. Several judges said they thought these smiles indicated "friendliness," "happiness," and even "joking." The judges who correctly chose Picture 1 interpreted these smiles differently. These judges read the smiles as the kind that may accompany polite conversation. One woman said, "In Picture 2, the bearded man's smile looks forced and professional, as if he hasn't been around the person very much—in Picture 1, the bearded man has a relaxed and fatherly look." A second woman said, "Parents don't smile so much with their own."

The relatively few judges who chose the right answer to this question thought that Picture 1 showed a more important relationship than Picture 2. I think the comments of these judges reflect their view of the sometimes complicated nature of kinship. One woman said, "The two men in Picture 1 seem more familiar with each other." Another woman said, "It looks as though they're having a family talk in Picture 1, while in Picture 2 it looks like they've just met." A third woman thought the men were having a "heavy conversation" in Picture 1, and a fourth woman thought they were "having an argument."

For judges who chose the correct answer, a key feature of Picture 1 is its intensity. One man commented that the two men in Picture 1 are "looking into each other's eyes," and another man said, "There is a certain intensity or sense of involvement in their eyes." Another judge's comment may reflect something in these pictures or else in the judge's own family background. This judge, a woman, said, "It's the intense one—the stereotypic view of father and son isn't usually laughing." Finally, I would like to think that one judge was accurate when she said, "The older man seems so much more *concerned* in Picture 1—there is a real feeling of communication and relationship in the way they look at each other."

Summary: The Beholder's Eye, Social Resemblance, and Kinship Scripts

The photographs in this chapter are all about parents, children, and the bonds of kinship. By answering the social intelligence questions in this chapter, our judges showed that there are several different types of kinship clues, and that many of these clues can be read successfully from photographs. The judges' answers also indicate that some kinship clues are more reliable than others. Despite popular belief to the contrary, I think this chapter demonstrates that appearance clues—our physical inheritance from our kinfolk—are unreliable. At least in the photographs in this chapter, physical resemblance was a poor basis for identifying parents and children.

I call this the problem of the "beholder's eye." I think the problem with physical resemblance is that it is only apparent after the fact. If we know that two people are related, then we can see (or think we see) striking similarities between them. This is the beholder's eye, and it can see similarities that may or may not be there. The obvious problem is that we can "see" physical similarities between almost any two people, whether they are related or not. In several of the questions in this chapter, some judges claimed to see a physical resemblance in one direction, while other judges claimed to see precisely the opposite. The beholder's eye is so strong that it can produce some embarrassing mistakes. I once told a woman how much she looked like her father only to be informed, rather icily, that he was her stepfather! So much for physical resemblance.

In trying to read these photographs, our judges were able to make much better use of social inheritance clues. I think parents and children do tend to bear a *social* resemblance to each other. They frequently share the same lifestyle, social class, taste in clothes, diet, and perhaps also beliefs and values. With all these things in common, it is not surprising that parents and children may seem similar.

Sometimes, perhaps unconsciously, we may mistake social resemblance for physical resemblance. We may think we see a similarity between two people's faces when we are really being influenced by social inheritance clues. In two of the questions in this chapter, page 107 and page 109, our judges had only individual photographs to go on. With no interaction clues available, our judges had to try to identify the young man's father and the young woman's mother using only the clues of physical and social inheritance. The accuracy of our judges' answers shows that they managed to do this quite successfully, and I think their answers reveal that they were reading a blend of clues to both physical and social resemblance.

In addition, the social intelligence questions in this chapter provide strong evidence that the very best clues to kinship are interaction clues. I think that we recognize a bond of kinship not so much from the way two people look, as from the way they interact. The qualities of our relationships translate into subtle but detectable interaction scripts. These scripts provide the raw data for our social intelligence. The way we look at, stand near, touch, or hold someone reveals something terribly important about our relationship. These behaviors reveal what we feel we have a right to expect from another person, and also what this person expects from us. These subtle behaviors are the nonverbal "signatures" of our kinship relationships. Parents and children interact as if they are performing complementary roles, and it is this performance that reveals that two people are parent and child.

Our photographs also indicate that a performance of the kinship script is very difficult to fake. When our judges were shown the picture on page 105, for example, they had no trouble identifying which of the two women on the bench was the children's mother. The important clues were interaction clues; the mother's interaction with the boys looked "right," and the other woman's interaction simply looked "wrong." Deciding that something looks right is an important part of social intelligence, since I think this is what allows us to interpret the behavior we see.

In most of the photographs in this chapter, the parents and children look right because they are—perhaps without thinking—following a kinship script. When they interact, they behave according to a script they have never read, but which they know by heart. Almost all of us know our parts in this kinship script. Fathers know how to be fathers, mothers know how to be mothers, and all but the very youngest children also "know" how children behave toward their parents. We all can perform these roles flawlessly with the right people—for example, fathers act like fathers when they are with their own children. When we are not with the right people, however, the performance is unconvincing. I think this is how our judges could tell that the woman on page 117 was not the boy's mother. She has children of her own, but this picture did not look right because she can only perform the mother script convincingly with her own children.

Finally, I would like to say an additional word about when an interaction looks right. Whenever we interact with another person, we make a great many decisions, and we probably make them unconsciously. We decide how close to stand to the person, whether to touch them, whether to look in their eyes, what to say, what words to use, what tone of voice to use, and how long the interaction should last. We may make hundreds of these unconscious decisions even in the most simple interaction. We probably make each of these decisions according to our relationship with a person; for example, we may decide to use a different voice with our parents than with our friends.

These hundreds of minute decisions are what make an interaction look and sound right. For this reason, social interaction is so complex that it defies piecemeal description. I suppose that every verbal and nonverbal detail of a five-minute conversation could be described—every word, gesture, eye movement, change of position, tone of voice—but it might require several volumes of painstaking observations. Fortunately, this kind of microscopic description is unnecessary. The beauty of social intelligence is that we can understand an interaction without being able to describe it. We can tell when two people are interacting like father and son, even if we cannot describe the hundreds of specific details that led to our interpretation. Looking "right" may be too complex a matter to explain, but it is a quality that our social intelligence allows us to recognize.

6 SIGNS OF POWER AND COMPETITION

The relationships we have discussed so far involve our intimates and kinsfolk. For most of us, however, life involves many other people as well. We interact with people at work, and some of the most enjoyable relationships in life are certainly the ones we build and maintain with friends.

In this chapter, I would like to consider two aspects of these relationships: power and competition. Almost all of us have experienced both. Most of us have been on the "receiving end" of a power relationship at some point in our lives. We may have worked under another person's supervision, served in some branch of the military, filed a request with some government authority, or simply obeyed a policeman. In our youth, all of us were told what to do by teachers and parents. In turn, some of us have experienced the other side of power relationships as well. We may have had our own employees, students, younger colleagues, and children. Since almost all organizations in our society have some kind of hierarchy, power relationships are unavoidable.

All of us have also known competition. At some point in our lives, we may have competed with someone in a game, on a test, at work, or even for some person's love. Competition may be one of the dominant themes in our culture. Siblings compete for a parent's approval, athletes compete for victory, corporations compete for markets, lawyers compete for verdicts, and even scientists compete for discoveries.

In recent years, there have been conscious efforts to limit some of the effects of power and competition. In a few corporations, employees and management have tried to make certain decisions jointly rather than in a "top-down" manner. Similarly, some schools have experimented with cooperative classrooms, and a few universities have adopted pass/fail or even ungraded curricula. For most of us, however, power and competition continue to be an important and inescapable fact of life.

Power and competition can have an important effect on our interaction with others. Again, I think there are social scripts that influence both what we say and what we do. I think there is a power script and also a competition script, and an understanding of these scripts may contribute to our social intelligence.

The power script involves both verbal and nonverbal behavior. These are the "signs" of power, and I believe they can be read. For example, in chapter 3 we discussed one gesture of power, the shoulder hold. A corporation president can put his or her arm around the shoulder of a lower-ranking employee, but the reverse is unthinkable. I imagine that this one-way shoulder hold is also found between teachers and students, coaches and athletes, and parents and children.

The power script has many other elements. One excellent sign of power is the "interruption license." In almost any conversation, interruptions usually involve a more powerful person interrupting a less powerful person. I suspect that this part of the power script is largely unconscious, but it appears to be extremely consistent. In an organization, the interruption license seems to follow the organizational hierarchy. Presidents do not hesitate to interrupt vice-presidents, vice-presidents interrupt assistant vice-presidents, and so on down the hierarchy.

Recent research suggests that the interruption license is also found in everyday conversations. Sociologists have recorded and studied conversations between men and women, and they have discovered that the majority of interruptions involve a man interrupting a woman. This seems to reflect the distribution of power between the two sexes. The interruption license can provide an intriguing social intelligence clue. The next time you observe a conversation, try to make a mental note of who interrupts whom. In any conversation, you may notice that one person does not hesitate to interrupt others, while some people passively submit to these interruptions. These interruption patterns can provide important clues about the relative power of each person.

There are also spatial signs of power. Sociologists have found that people tend to stand farther from people who are high in rank or status. For example, on the night John F. Kennedy was elected President, his friends and advisers were watching the election returns, and they suddenly realized that their friend had just become the President of the United States. At that moment, according to one adviser, their spatial interaction with Kennedy changed dramatically—the advisers moved back a "respectful" distance and formed a sort of circle around Kennedy. This formal distance was in response to the tremendous power Kennedy had just acquired. Another spatial aspect of the power script involves seating position. At a rectangular table, the most powerful person is almost always seated at one end of the table, while less powerful people are seated along the sides of the table.

The power script also includes subtle visual clues. For example, psychologists have found that powerful people may listen to other people without looking at them. By contrast, less powerful people usually pay close "visual attention" when listening to a powerful person. Visual attention seems to be a gesture of respect in our culture, and powerful people may feel free to make this gesture or not.

Specific nonverbal details may also be signs of power. Sociologist Allan Mazur believes that when two people interact, the power relationship between them is reflected in their eyebrows. Mazur suggests that elevated eyebrows indicate deference, while lowered eyebrows reflect power. In these very simple drawings, for example, which "face" looks more dominant? I think it is the one on the right. The face with the raised eyebrows looks meek or submissive in comparison to the more aggressive, determined, or "powerful" expression conveyed by the lowered eyebrows of the other face.

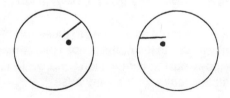

I think there is also a unique social script for competition. Most of us have seen this competition script performed so many times that I think we tend to take it for granted. In games and athletic contests, winners and losers in our society tend to follow an elaborate, ritualized interaction. After a competition, etiquette calls for both the winner and loser to praise one another extravagantly. A "good loser" is one who will compliment the winner and say that the winner deserved the victory. Good losers are not expected to attribute their loss to bad luck, to make excuses for their defeat, or to belittle the skills of the victor.

Winners also follow an extremely strict competition script. If anything, the winner's script is even more rigid than the loser's. In our society, winners are under tremendous social pressure to disguise the triumphant joy they are certain to feel at winning. This joy can be expressed to a teammate, but not to an opponent. For example, imagine a Wimbledon tennis match in which the victor jumps the net, runs over to the vanquished opponent, and says, "I'm so glad that I beat you!" This would be considered bad form or poor sportsmanship. Instead, the winner is likely to say that it was a difficult match that could have gone either way, that luck made the difference, or that the loser just had a bad day. While the "good" loser is expected to say that skill determined the outcome, a "gracious" winner is obligated to attribute the victory to luck. I suspect that these remarks may be just the opposite of what the loser and winner really think.

One of the most sacred rules of the winner's script is that the winner cannot belittle the loser's ability. This kind of criticism is permissible *before* a competition, but not after. Imagine a professional basketball coach who has just won the NBA championship in a seven game play-off series. It would be unthinkable for the winning coach to say "We beat them because they are worse than we are." The victorious coach may say that his players won because of their greater effort, team work, endurance, or even luck—but he is unlikely to say that his players simply have more ability.

There are a number of exceptions to these rules. Sometimes, a competitor may refuse to follow the script. I think these exceptions prove just how powerful the competition script really is. If a famous professional athlete says, "I won because I am a much better player," the remark is likely to attract media attention and provoke controversy. This part of the competition script is fascinating because, in some cases, it is obvious to everyone that the winner really is much better. While commentators and fans are free to say this, however, the winner is not.

Sports fans appear to love and admire the great athlete who is humble, but they have no affection for the equally great athlete who is not. It is almost as if the humble athlete makes it possible for others to heap praise upon him or her, while the proud athlete robs the fans of the chance to "participate" in the victory in this way. Perhaps this is why many fans dislike the great athlete who knows, and says, just how great he or she is. When an athlete like this is defeated, some fans and commentators may say, with apparent satisfaction, that he or she has been "humiliated." I think they mean that an athlete who would not play the competition script voluntarily has been humbled against his or her will. To some, this may seem like a deserved punishment for a proud athlete who has refused to abide by the traditional competition script.

These loser and winner scripts should provide useful clues for our social intelligence. If we hear two people discussing a game they have just played, we may be able to guess who won. The player who refers to his or her good luck is almost certainly the winner. In addition, I think there are also nonverbal signs of victory. I have noticed that the loser of a contest may show a "nonverbal deference"—an averted gaze, a lowered head, a catch in the voice, and a wan or forced smile.

Can the deference of the loser be recognized? After all, winners struggle to conceal their joy and pride, and losers struggle to conceal their disappointment and resentment. Despite the ritual of the competition script, I think there are visible clues. I think the real emotions of the winners and losers "leak" out, despite their efforts at concealment. These leaked emotions are clues that our social intelligence can allow us to detect and read.

Robin Akert and I once videotaped people immediately after they had competed against one another. In one case, two men had just played a game of "one-on-one" basketball. On the next page is a picture of the two men along with a transcript of their conversation about the game.

MAN ON THE LEFT: I, uh, used too much muscle. And, uh, there's
one time in particular when I hit Jack in the stomach with
my elbow, which, uh, could have been avoided. Other
times, I hit him, but it wasn't quite as uh . . . I, I guess,
intentional as that, as that, that one was. Uh, I would try to
work on lay-ups if I did it again, so I, I could practice
breaking through, see if I could get under the basket
instead of having to rely on outside shots.

MAN ON THE RIGHT: Well, my mistake was before the game. I
spent a half an hour working out and I, uh, could hardly
keep up with David some of the time. But on the other
hand, I hit some nice long ones. So. . . .

Can you spot the winner? It is the man on the left, the one
without a shirt. We showed the videotape to several hundred
college students, and 64 percent correctly identified the winner.
Many of these student judges were struck by the apologetic tone of
the winner's remarks. The man on the left does seem to express the
polite humility that the competition script requires of winners in our
society. This is even more striking on the videotape than in the
transcript. On the videotape, the man on the left seems positively
embarrassed by his victory. The accuracy of our judges shows that

they were able to decode this performance of the competition script correctly.

The social intelligence items in this chapter concern various signs of power and competition. In many ways, these photographs contain fewer clues than we would have in actual situations. A photograph can indicate that two people are having a conversation, but it does not allow us to detect clues like the interruption license. With only a photograph to go on, we cannot hear a competitor mention luck or detect a power relationship by noticing the length of each person's visual attention. Despite these limitations, I believe that certain qualities of power and competition can be inferred from photographs in many cases.

The following social intelligence questions show that our judges were very successful at reading the nonverbal evidence in the photographs. The photographs are labelled as they were when the items were tested. Here is the first photograph.

Person 1   Person 2

These two women are co-workers. Who is in charge?

    a. Person 1

    b. Person 2

Answer: b. Person 2

Accuracy (50.0%)

Women	Men	Total
81.2%	92.0%	86.6%

This simple photograph seems to have captured an entire constellation of power relationship clues. The correct answer is that the woman on the right is the person in charge. A surprising 86 percent of our judges were able to interpret the power relationship, and for some reason men were significantly more accurate than women on this question.

Our judges seemed to see several different signs of power. One woman said the woman with the long hair looks "as if she is listening very carefully," and another woman thought she looks "positively anxious." Several judges said they thought this woman was "getting instructions" from her superior. One man commented on the position of this woman's eyebrows. He said, "Her eyebrows are raised in acknowledgment—does this reflect her submission?" This observant judge seems to have stumbled onto the eyebrow power clue discussed earlier in this chapter.

Other judges commented on the "authoritative" appearance of the short-haired woman. Judges said she looks "older," "more sophisticated," and "serious." I was interested to see that women judges were more likely than men to notice differences in dress and appearance. Several women said that the "boss's" scarf makes her look like a "career woman," and one judge said, "Her hair is obviously done professionally."

Most judges thought it was significant that this woman is "elevated" above the other woman, and judges said that it appears as if she is "talking down" to the woman on the left. One man described the short-haired woman as having a "confident tilt of the head," and another man said she looks "condescending." I think that the comments of one woman judge touched on the visual attention clue discussed earlier. This judge noticed that the woman on the left seems careful to keep her eyes on the short-haired woman, while her superior seems indifferent to eye contact. Finally, I think my favorite comment was made by the woman who guessed correctly that the short-haired woman is the boss and said simply, "She gives off manager vibes."

Person 1

Person 2

These two men just played basketball. Who won?

    a. **Person 1**

    b. **Person 2**

Answer: b. Person 2

Accuracy (50.0%)

Women	Men	Total
80.4%	72.6%	76.7%

Three out of four judges guessed correctly that the winner in this photograph is the man on the right. Some of our judges were struck by very simple clues. For example, several judges mentioned that the man on the right is holding the ball. One man said, "He appears to be in control of the ball and thus *was* in control of the game." Another man said, "It always seems like the winner owns the ball—it was probably his idea to play in the first place." A third judge noted, "He is holding the ball like he is ready for more." One woman even commented on the way this man holds the ball. She said, "He holds it very lightly, with the finesse and confidence of a winner—it's dexterity and not just a clutch."

Most of our judges also thought they detected the subtle details of a competition script. Both of the men in the photograph are smiling broadly, but are these two smiles the same? Most of our judges thought they saw a difference. One woman said the man on the left is "fake smiling," and another judge said this man "has an air of embarrassment about him, as if he was reluctant to pose." I was impressed by the comment of the woman judge who said, "The man on the left is smiling all right, but his eyes show that he has lost." Another woman said that the loser has "wandering eyes" compared to the "victorious glint" in the eyes of the winner. One of our judges noted some microscopic details. He said, "Look at the winner's smile—it is more genuine because the creases around the eyes are more pronounced, and the lips are drawn further back from the teeth."

I think that this photograph provides a textbook demonstration that there are smiles and then there are *smiles*. The smile of the winner seems spontaneous, while the smile of the loser looks performed. I imagine that both of these men were trying to behave according to the competition script—the winner trying to disguise his triumph by looking humble, and the loser trying to conceal his disappointment with the generous grin of a good loser. About 77 percent of the judges, however, could tell who had won. I think this means that the real feelings of the two men "leaked" despite their best acting efforts.

Person 1   Person 2

These two men are co-workers in a bookstore. Who is in charge?

    a. Person 1

    b. Person 2

Answer: a. Person 1

Accuracy (50.0%)

Women	Men	Total
66.0%	63.3%	64.6%

As about two thirds of our judges guessed, the owner of the bookstore is the man on the left. One of the clues is simply that this man looks older, and it is generally true that people in power tend to be older than their subordinates. As one of our women judges said, "I assume that older people are in charge, although I know it's not *always* true." Judges also said the man on the left looks "neater," "mature," "responsible," "distinguished," and "more conserva- tive." One judge also thought the store owner looks like an "in- charge" person, and one woman said, "He looks tough, like a manager."

Some judges also thought they detected signs of a power script. A few judges commented on how far apart the two men are standing. One woman said, "This is definitely a work relationship and not a friendship." Another woman said that the man with the beard looks "too nervous," and another judge said, "This man's folded arms represent uneasiness." I think there also may be clues in the store owner's face. One woman said his face has the "relaxed look of someone who knows he has authority." When I look at this photograph, I am struck by what I see as the wry smile on the store owner's face. Whatever this expression "really" is, I don't think it is deference, and two thirds of our judges seemed to agree.

Person 1   Person 2

These two women just played a game of racketball. Who won?

    a. Person 1

    b. Person 2

Answer: b. Person 2

Accuracy (50.0%)

Women	Men	Total
85.2%	**77.7%**	**81.7%**

This seems to be a vivid portrait of competition; eight out of ten judges correctly identified the woman on the right as the winner. Judges said this woman shows more "spark" and looks more "excited," "alive," and "energetic." Several judges cited differences in posture. One woman said, "Person 2 holds her head up and looks aggressively jubilant, while Person 1 shows the slumped posture of defeat."

Our judges also thought they detected an important difference between the women's smiles. One woman said, "On Person 2, it looks like the grin comes naturally—but Person 1 has eyebrows uplifted in the middle like it's a little painful to smile." Another judge said, "Person 2's openmouthed smile looks cocky, triumphant, and exhilarated, while Person 1 looks like she's forcing a smile—her eyes look tired and defeated." This comment is similar to something a judge said about the smiles of the basketball players on page 137, and I think it may be an important social intelligence clue. I think fake smiles do not reach the person's eyes. A fake smile "flashes" in the mouth and lower part of the face, while a real smile is strong enough to change the eyes and the upper part of the face as well.

I think one of the most fascinating comments concerns the winner script we discussed earlier. This judge, a man, thought he saw Person 2 struggling hard to mask her triumphant feelings with humility. He said, "Maybe I am just expressing my own problem here, but it seems to me that the woman on the right looks like she wants to be humble but doesn't know how."

Judges also thought that Person 2 looks more "sportsy." Several judges commented on her "jock" headband, and one man said, "She seems better equipped for the sport, while the other woman wears 'pretty' clothing." Another woman was even more observant in her comment. She said, "I have never known a good athlete to play in a Mexican shirt—they don't keep you cool." Finally, I think the competition clues in this picture are summarized succinctly by the man who said, "Person 1 looks beat, and Person 2's mouth seems to be saying, 'Hooray! I won.' "

Team 1   Team 2

These four men just played a game of tennis. Which team won?

      a. Team 1

      b. Team 2

Answer: b. Team 2

Accuracy (50.0%)

Women	Men	Total
15.7%	10.5%	13.3%

This is one of the most misleading photographs in this book—only about 13 percent of our judges picked Team 2 as the winners. I think there are a number of reasons for this. One of the most striking details in this picture is that one man on the winning team has his tongue hanging out. This is the kind of odd behavioral detail that photographs sometimes capture. A camera shutter that opens for only a fraction of a second can record fleeting "slices" of behavior that our eyes may miss or be trained to overlook. We all have seen photographs that record blinks, sneezes, startled glances, or other momentary behavior. These pictures look "funny" because we tend to suppress our awareness of these behaviors in everyday life, and these photographs provide vivid reminders of what we have suppressed.

In this picture, our camera captured a protruding tongue. Most judges drew the wrong conclusion about this. For example, one man said, "The person on the left in Team 2 is exhausted, with his tongue out, which indicates that the other team wore him out." Another judge said that this tennis player seems to be saying, "Blah, I'm tired out." One woman even thought that he is "sticking out his tongue in disgust" at the way he played. One judge may have been speaking from experience when he said, "This man looks like he lost and has to pick up the tab for the beer."

Although most judges were misled by the clue of the protruding tongue, a few read this detail differently. One man said, "It takes hard work to win (his tongue is hanging out)." I think an intriguing analysis was made by the woman who said, "The man with his tongue out looks like a ham—he may be trying to pretend that it was a rough game, although he probably enjoyed every minute of it and loved winning." I think this judge is absolutely right, and that the protruding tongue is this man's winner script. It is his way of appearing humble about his victory and saying, nonverbally, "Boy, that was a tough game, and we were very lucky to beat them."

A few judges used other clues to reach the correct answer. A number of them explained their accurate answers by saying that they thought the man with the beard in Team 1 does not look genuinely pleased. I enjoyed the comment of the woman who said, "The bearded guy is gesturing with his racket as if to say, 'Laugh at me and I'll break your face.'"

For the most part, however, our judges were misled. In addition to the clue of the tongue, some judges said that the men on Team 1 are taller and look more athletic. I suppose this is a "logical" guess, but it just happens to be wrong in this case. I will say more about the difference between logic and social intelligence in the final chapter.

Woman Left   Woman Right

These two women work together. One is a sales clerk, and one is the manager. Which one is the manager?

    a. the woman on the left

    b. the woman on the right

Answer: b. the woman on the right

Accuracy (50.0%)

Women	Men	Total
68.8%	75.3%	72.0%

I think this is not an easily read photograph, but almost three quarters of our judges correctly chose the woman on the right as the manager. Both women work in a rather fashionable clothing store, but the woman on the right is indeed in charge. I think we can see the visual attention clue again in this picture. The employee seems very attentive to the manager, but the manager does not return the gaze. One judge said, "The woman on the left appears to be listening to instructions." Another judge said this woman "has her lips tight as if she is anxious." One man said simply, "She is displaying deferential treatment."

There are also appearance clues in this picture. Judges said the manager looks "older," "responsible," "reserved," and "authoritative." Several judges commented on the more "executive style" dress of the woman on the right. Some of our judges thought hairstyles were a significant clue. Judges called the employee's hairstyle "too youthful" or "too Bohemian" to be worn by a manager. I think the *contrast* between these two women is itself an important clue. I am not sure that our judges would have regarded the woman on the left as "too Bohemian" to be a manager if they saw only her picture. But when the two women are compared, the contrast appears to be a decisive clue.

Person 1   Person 2

These two men have just arm wrestled. Who won?

    a. Person 1

    b. Person 2

Answer: b. Person 2

Accuracy (50.0%)

Women	Men	Total
83.3%	80.6%	82.1%

Our judges did extremely well on this final competition question. As the answer picture shows, the man in the tank-top shirt out-muscled and over-powered his companion. Eight out of ten judges correctly chose this man as the winner. This excellent performance indicates that the photograph of the two men contains some vivid competition script clues.

Our judges cited dozens of details. Some judges were impressed that Person 2 is looking directly into the camera, while Person 1 seems to be looking at the winner. One woman said, "The direct gaze at the camera denotes a feeling of superiority." A man said, "Person 1 looks like his ego is hurt," and one woman even said, "Person 1 looks like he's about to cry, and he's avoiding looking into the camera." I do not agree with her analysis—I think the loser is simply embarrassed and is staring, perhaps resentfully, at the winner. As one man said, "Person 1 looks like he wants revenge."

Almost all the judges were struck by the "strong," "proud" look on the face of the winner. Another man said, "He's giving us the 'hard guy' look." Some of the comments show an impressive attention to anatomical details. One man said, "Person 2 has a thrust-out jaw (showing teeth, as in a challenge) and narrowed eyes—he wouldn't be very aggressive like this if he lost." A woman said "Person 2 has his chin jutted out, with his mouth and eyes held like he's saying, 'Hey, I'm tough.' "

Several judges used the word *macho* to describe the winner's nonverbal behavior. One woman said, "He has his tongue right behind his front teeth, squared shoulders, etc.—this is very macho." Another woman said, "Even his shirt is more macho!" Other judges said the winner looks "jockier," "cocky," "sure of himself," "stronger," and "cool like a winner." One man used slang to describe the winner, saying, "He's acting real bad."

The variety of comments indicates that there are many competition clues in this photograph, and our judges' accuracy shows that these clues of victory and defeat are very "legible."

Summary: Reading the Signs of Power and Competition

The photographs in this chapter are all about the signs of power and competition. These signs appear to follow a reliable script. As we discussed at the beginning of this chapter, the power script includes the shoulder hold, the interruption license, spatial distancing, visual attention, and even something as incredibly specific as the elevation of a person's eyebrow. The competition script consists of an elaborate ritual in which winners and losers attempt to mask their true emotions. Despite this formal ritual, the real feelings of the winner and loser often "leak" out, and these leaks are important social intelligence clues.

The photographs in this chapter can reveal only *visual* aspects of the power script and competition script. Despite this constraint, our judges in general were extremely accurate in their efforts to decode the power and competition clues in our photographs. I think this demonstrates that visual clues can be extraordinarily eloquent. On the face of it, I think the performance of our judges is nothing less than astonishing. Again in this chapter, our judges were able to tell something important about total strangers using only an incredibly small scrap of information: a single photograph showing no more than a fraction of one second of these people's lives.

I think that this is a remarkable feat of interpretation. For me, this constitutes the "miracle" of social intelligence. I have tried to explore the comments of our judges to discover *how* our social intelligence operates. I have tried to learn how people decode specific clues, how they contrast and combine different details, how they read messages in a person's face and body, and how they manage to process these hundreds of details into a single social intelligence conclusion.

When we examine what other people have said about each picture in this book, we have a rare opportunity to share unique aspects of their social intelligence. I think this sharing gives us a priceless chance to increase our own social intelligence. In the next chapter, I want to describe a simple method we can use to try to continue improving our social intelligence in everyday life.

7 IMPROVING YOUR SOCIAL INTELLIGENCE

When I decided to write this book, I hoped that we could discover not only specific social intelligence clues, but also new ways of seeing. Studying the photographs has enabled us to identify dozens of fascinating social intelligence clues including the shoulder hold, the waxy hand effect, social inheritance, and winner and loser scripts. These specific social intelligence clues are the central focus of this book. However, I think we can learn something else from the judges who looked at the photographs. Our judges' comments contain some general lessons that can help us to see people and their behavior in a new way. In this final chapter, I want to do two things. First, I want to describe what I think is an important difference between successful and unsuccessful ways of seeing people. Second, I want to describe a simple method that readers of this book can use in everyday life to continue improving their social intelligence.

After reading tens of thousands of comments, I have concluded that some ways of seeing are more successful than others. I am using the word *success* in the social intelligence sense of the word. A successful way of seeing is one that leads to *accurate* interpretations of people and their behavior. Since all the questions in this book have objectively correct answers, we have a solid bench mark that we can use to evaluate the accuracy of our judges' interpretations. Some of these judges were more successful than others. It seems to me that the successful and unsuccessful judges approached the social intelligence questions in different ways.

For want of better terms, I call these different styles of applying social intelligence the logical method and the inductive method. Although these are both methods of reasoning, I think there is an important difference between the approaches. Using the logical method, a person first makes a decision about the question and then looks selectively for clues in terms of this prior decision. Using the inductive method, a person examines the clues with as few preconceptions as possible and then tries to construct a decision based on a careful examination of the available evidence. The difference between these two styles of social intelligence is important because I think that the inductive approach is far more successful than the logical approach.

The difference between these two ways of seeing can be illustrated easily. In the question on page 137, for example, judges were asked to guess which of two men had won a basketball game. Most of our judges (76.7 percent) correctly identified the winner, and they seemed to do this inductively—by a careful examination of the two men's facial expressions and other clues. Judges who used a logical approach tended to be misled. One judge who chose the wrong man said, "I am guessing that Person 1 is the winner because he is taller." Since everyone knows that height is an advantage in basketball, I suppose that this is a logical decision. But it does not take into account the rich tapestry of social intelligence clues in the photograph. This judge missed the differences in the men's eyes, the contrast in their smiles, and many other details. In fact, since this judge based his answer solely on the relative height of the two men, he barely needed to look at the picture. The ultimate test of this judge's approach is whether it produces the right answer, and it does not. Despite the "logic" of looking at height, the shorter man won the game.

I think the problem with the logical approach is that it can reduce our ability to see all of the evidence. The logical approach can lead to a kind of "tunnel vision," where we see only what a special kind of reasoning leads us to expect. Clues that do not conform to these expectations tend to be overlooked. I think that judges who approached our photographs logically tried to fit what they saw to some personal or preconceived theory about human behavior. Looking only at the height of two basketball players is an example of this. This judge applied his height theory to the two basketball players without *really* looking at them.

There are many other examples of the failure of the logical approach. The following comments were made about several different photographs. The comments that follow have two things in common: They all reflect a logical style of social intelligence, and they all led these judges to the wrong conclusions.

"I don't think brothers and sisters of their age would play tennis together—my brother and I don't."

"This woman looks too young to have a husband or a child."

"This woman is the boy's mother because he is sitting on her lap, and children only sit on their own parent's lap."

"Mothers and their grown daughters don't have picnics together."

"I never smile like that when I am standing with *my* sister."

"It looks like these two people are standing in front of a house, so I guess they must be married."

"This man looks just like my uncle, and he owns a business too."

"Children always pose in front of their parents, so it must be the child on the right."

"These two people are the same age, so they must be married."

Some of these comments, like the one about brothers and sisters not playing tennis together, could have been made without even looking at the photographs. Each of these judges tried to apply some kind of personal theory or rule to the photographs. Unfortunately, these theories and rules seemed to obstruct the judges' view of the really important clues, because the judges who made these comments all chose the wrong answers to the questions.

I think the inductive approach is more successful because it is less restricted by theories, expectations, and rules. When we use the inductive approach, we are more likely to see *all* of a picture and not just the details that fit a preconceived logic. For this reason, the inductive approach is inherently more open-minded. When we "see" inductively, we examine all the clues we can detect and try to construct our interpretation from the ground up.

I think it is important to ask whether we can teach ourselves to see inductively. I am sure that this skill is not as simple or mechanical as, for example, learning the rules for playing checkers. Improving our social intelligence is obviously a complex task, and I think that a very special form of experience is probably the best teacher. However, I do think that there are a number of general guidelines that can help us learn to see inductively.

For one thing, it is critical for us to notice and really see the clues that are all around us. This may sound like a simple matter, but I believe that most of us have developed habits that lead us to do precisely the opposite. Even a brief interaction contains a bewildering number of potential clues including words, facial expressions, and gestures, and I think that most of us disregard or tune out most of this distracting "noise." In a conversation, for example, most of us have probably developed the habit of attending primarily to words, at the expense of nonverbal clues. Similarly, I think we tend to watch those who are speaking and ignore those who are silent. I think that these perceptual habits are unconscious and extremely powerful.

I received a dramatic and embarrassing lesson about perceptual habits a few years ago. My wife and I were having dinner at the house of our friends Bob and Maureen. The four of us were having a very animated conversation when the telephone rang. Maureen's parents were calling to speak with her, and after Maureen picked up the phone, I continued exchanging jokes and laughing with Bob. I cannot remember even looking at Maureen after she answered the phone, although she was standing near the table in plain view. Fortunately, not everyone in the room had the same perceptual habits. After a minute, my wife touched me on the arm and nodded toward Maureen. Tears were cascading down Maureen's cheeks, and her eyes were closed in wordless grief. We all fell silent and Bob went to Maureen's side. She hung up the phone, and we learned that her collie, a family pet for fourteen years, had just been struck by a car and killed. I felt stupid not to have seen Maureen's grief, and to have continued laughing with Bob. My preoccupation with the spoken word had made me insensitive to nonverbal clues happening only a few feet away.

In a different way, university teaching also has taught me how easy it is to notice only those who talk. In seminars, I frequently have received a brilliant paper from a student who has been nearly "invisible" in terms of his or her verbal participation in class discussions. Similarly, some of the most vocal participants sometimes submit a lackluster piece of work. This has taught me that only some of the things worth hearing are freely spoken, and that only some of the things freely spoken are worth hearing. As a result of these experiences, I now try to "scan" the faces of people who do not talk as well as listen to those who do.

Learning to see inductively is hard work. For one thing, I think we all start from the premise that we already know how to see, and after all, we all possess a social intelligence. The question is, however, whether we can become better judges of people and their behavior. In order to improve our social intelligence, I believe we must unshackle ourselves from perceptual habits we may have acquired over decades of our lives. These habits include our tendencies to alter or limit our perceptions to fit our preconceptions, to look at many clues without seeing some of them, to limit our attention to speakers and ignore silent behavior, and to prefer words to everything else. These habits can be modified, I believe, and the first step in this direction is to recognize that we have them. The next section describes a simple method that we can use in everyday life to exercise and try to improve our social intelligence.

Active Interpretation: A Method for Improving Your Social Intelligence

I have designed something called the "active interpretation method" for improving your social intelligence. This method is simple, easy to use, and I hope, interesting as well. I think of this method as a real-life version of the photographs and questions in this book. The basis of active interpretation is a procedure that people can use to create their own social intelligence questions. This method has just three simple steps:

1. Try to *recognize* a situation in which you have a chance to guess the answer to a social intelligence question. State the question.

2. Examine the available clues and answer your own question. *Commit* yourself to your answer, and make a mental note of the clues that influenced your answer.

3. Finally, try to invent a way to *test* your accuracy—try to find out if you are right or wrong.

These three steps were the foundation for the way I designed the social intelligence questions in this book. The real-life tests are, of course, more varied and complicated, but I believe that following these three simple active interpretation steps can help us to improve our social intelligence. As will be shown, all three of these steps are extremely important, and this method cannot be fully effective unless all three are completed.

Before explaining the theory behind active interpretation, I would like to illustrate this method with eight examples from my own experience. Most readers will be able to recognize in their own lives hundreds or even thousands of active interpretation opportunities as they occur. I present these eight examples only to illustrate the three steps of the active interpretation method.

Example 1. You enter a small café for lunch. On the way in, you see parked out front an enormous black and chrome Harley-Davidson motorcycle with a greatly extended front fork. The restaurant has five customers, and they are sitting at the luncheon counter. Recognizing an opportunity for a social intelligence question, you decide to guess which of the customers is the "biker." (This is Step 1 of the active interpretation method.) You choose a seat against the far wall, where you can see both the counter and the motorcycle outside the window. Using a combination of discreet staring and furtive glances, you notice that one of the men at the counter is wearing a headband and heavy boots that have scuff marks on the top of one toe. You choose this man as the biker (Step 2), and then you order lunch and wait. Finally, when one of the five customers leaves on the Harley, you find out if your social intelligence guess was right or wrong (Step 3).

Example 2. In today's mail, you have received what looks like four Christmas cards. Your address is handwritten on all four envelopes, and none of the letters shows a return address. You recognize an opportunity for a social intelligence question, and you decide to guess whether the writing was done by men or women (Step 1). Without opening the envelopes, you study the handwriting on each one and notice that three of the addresses are written in a very neat, regular hand, while the fourth is a scrawl. You guess that the neat handwriting was done by women, and the scrawl by a man. To prevent losing track of your guesses, you mark the four envelopes with an *M* or *W* (Step 2). Finally, you open the envelopes to see how many of your guesses are right (Step 3). If three or all four of your guesses are correct, you are doing better than chance accuracy.

Example 3. When you bring some merchandise to the checkout counter in a liquor store, you see that another customer has placed three identical bottles of wine on the counter. The customer is not there, and you assume that he or she has gone back for some additional item. You notice that the wine has a prestigious and costly label. Looking around the store, you see six customers, and you decide to guess which person is buying the expensive wine (Step 1). You examine the six customers discreetly and you notice that one is wearing what appears to be an expensive leather coat. You choose this person (Step 2), and by waiting until the purchaser of the wine returns to the counter, you find out if your guess is correct (Step 3).

Example 4. It is a warm Saturday in spring, and you have taken your four-year-old to the park. On the bench next to yours, two adults are with a very young child. You recognize a social intelligence opportunity, and decide to try to guess the age and sex of the child (Step 1). You notice that the child still has ruddy cheeks and "baby fat" in the cheeks, and you see that the child is wearing a dark sweater. You guess that the child is a ten-month-old boy (Step 2). Since it is permissible in our society for complete strangers to exchange information about their children, you decide to start a conversation. You avoid a direct question about gender by asking, "How old is your baby?" It seems to me that this is a well-chosen opening line. If the parents respond by saying, "He's eleven months," you can grade your guess as very good (Step 3).

Example 5. The phone rings when you are visiting a friend's house, and your friend answers it. You decide to try to guess whether the person on the other end of the phone is a man or woman, and also what sort of relationship this person has with your friend (Step 1). You notice that your friend seems very involved in the conversation. Your friend's voice is animated and cheerful, and your friend's end of the conversation seems very positive but not at all deferential. You guess that the caller is a good friend of the opposite sex, and about the same age as your friend (Step 2). When the conversation is over, there are two ways you can find out if you are right. The indirect way is to ask very casually, "Who was that?" Your friend's answer probably will reveal whether you are right or wrong. The direct way is to be more open about your interest in social intelligence. You can explain that you are trying to learn to read clues from people's voices. Tell your friend what you have guessed, and ask whether you are right or wrong (Step 3).

Example 6. Your sister Tricia and brother-in-law Larry invite you to a party at their house. They explain that most of the other people at the party will be from the corporation where Larry works. These are people you have never met before. When you arrive at the crowded party, you decide to try to guess which of the guests is Larry's boss (Step 1). You know that Larry's boss is a man, but you don't know what he looks like. After looking at all the guests, you notice three slightly older men who seem to be dressed somewhat more conservatively than the other guests. You think that one of these men is probably the boss, but which one? On the other side of the room, one of the three men is surrounded by several younger guests, who stand at a respectful distance. This cluster includes your brother-in-law, and you notice that Larry's eyebrows are raised, and that he seems careful to maintain eye contact with the older man. Larry also seems to punctuate the conversation by nodding his head whenever the older man speaks. You decide that this must be Larry's boss (Step 2). Your decision made, you take your sister aside to find out whether you are right or wrong (Step 3).

Example 7. You are teaching a college seminar. It is the first meeting of the class, and there are twenty students in the room. You ask the students to give their names and say a few words about the interests that have led them to choose this class. One of the students, a young woman, stares intently at the other students as they speak. You also observe that she glances covertly at the open notebooks of the people on either side of her. When it is her turn to speak, you learn that her name is Carie Squires. She stares directly at you while she speaks, and you notice something subtly but distinctly unusual about her voice. You recognize a social intelligence opportunity, and the clues you have observed lead you to guess that Carie is largely or completely deaf (Step 1 and Step 2). As part of the course requirements, the students in the seminar are expected to discuss their research interests with you during the first week of the course. Carie comes to your office to discuss her research plans, and you try to think of a way to test the accuracy of your guess. You rule out the possibility of asking her directly. The question would seem bizarre if you are wrong, and if you are right you might undercut her pride in being able to function well with her deafness concealed. Clearly, a discreet test is required. At the end of the conversation, Carie leaves your office, and you watch her walk down the hall. When she is about fifteen feet away, you call out in a very loud voice, "Oh, Carie, one more thing." She keeps walking (Step 3).

Example 8. You are with a friend in San Francisco's China-town, driving down Waverly Place. You are headed for one of your favorite restaurants, and you are looking for a parking place on the crowded street. Suddenly, you see a man climb into the cab of a beat-up pickup truck parked in a metered space ahead on the right. Your hopes soar, but there is a Mercedes-Benz in front of you and the Mercedes stops, waiting to take the space. Your hopes fade. Just then, the driver of the parked truck jumps out of the cab, and looking right at the driver of the Mercedes, he points the index finger of his right hand straight up in the air. With an angry squeal of its tires, the Mercedes drives off. You decide to try to guess the intentions of the truck driver (Step 1). You noticed that the truck driver's facial expression was pleasant and not aggressive as he held up his hand. Having observed something else, you say to your friend, "Wrong finger." You decide that the truck driver was giving the Mercedes driver the "one minute" sign rather than an obscene gesture, so you decide to wait (Step 2). The truck driver raises the hood of his pickup, tightens his battery cable, jumps back in the cab, and drives away (Step 3). You take the empty parking space, which happens to be right across from your favorite restaurant. Very convenient.

These are just eight examples of how the active interpretation method can be used to exercise your social intelligence. In everyday life, you probably encounter dozens of similar opportuni-

ties. Conscious practice can help you recognize these opportunities, and you can try to follow the three simple steps of the active
interpretation method. First, formulate a social intelligence question. Second, commit yourself to an answer for your own question.
Third, try to think of a way to test the accuracy of your answer.

The third step is extremely important, and in some ways it is
the key to the success of the entire method. If we do not test our
own accuracy, we fail to go beyond conventional curiosity, and we
pass up a chance for a valuable lesson in social intelligence. It is
common to become curious about someone and to make some sort
of guess about this person, but most people never find out if their
guesses are right or wrong. I think this omission prevents people
from improving their social intelligence.

Two analogies will help explain why the third step—finding out
if your interpretations are accurate—is so important. The first of
these is a sports analogy involving basketball. Imagine two people,
Person A and Person B, who are trying to improve their accuracy at
making shots from the foul line. Person A spends one hour a day
practicing foul shots and tries to correct his tendencies to over-
shoot, undershoot, and so on. Person B also spends an hour a day
practicing foul shots, but with one difference. Just as the basketball
leaves his fingertips, Person B closes his eyes. Person B, therefore, never finds out if his shots go into the basket or miss. Even if
Person B thinks that a shot has missed, he cannot know exactly
what was wrong with it. Under these conditions, which person do
you think will show the most improvement? It is, of course, Person
A. Person B cannot improve his accuracy because he does not
even know when he has missed.

Making interpretations without testing the accuracy of your
social intelligence is like taking basketball shots with your eyes
closed. In both cases, accuracy cannot be improved. There is a
sound scientific reason for this. If you know that you have missed (a
basketball shot or an interpretation), you can learn to avoid making
the same mistake again. To use the vocabulary of the psychology
of learning, you can "negatively reinforce" the sequence that
produced the inaccuracy. On the other hand, if you find out that you
were accurate, you can consolidate your accuracy by making the
way you did it a part of your learned repertoire. In other words, you

can "positively reinforce" the things you did that made you accurate. Either way, you can only improve your skill if you know whether or not your attempts are accurate.

The second analogy seems very different on the surface, but I believe the same scientific principle is involved. This analogy concerns bird populations. I must confess that I know very little about this subject, but I have read that teams of naturalists and volunteers conduct a periodic census of various bird populations. They do this by stationing observers in different locations to count birds as they sit in trees, gather in fields, and fly overhead. Imagine yourself crouching in a flooded marsh as a dark cloud of ducks flew by. Could you give a confident estimate of the number of birds? How could you try to improve your accuracy at making this kind of census?

The answer to this accuracy problem is uncannily similar to the analogy of our basketball players. The key step, again, is that people must be able to learn whether their attempts are accurate or not. Bird census takers train in the following way. They sit at a table with a bag of uncooked rice. Reaching into the bag, they quickly scatter a small handful of rice on the table. In a single glance, they make an instant estimate of the number of rice kernels—say, 125. So far, this is just like taking a foul shot or making a social intelligence interpretation. If these census takers did no more, I doubt that they would ever become more accurate. However, they complete the key step of counting the actual number of rice kernels on the table. This tells the census takers whether an estimate was too low, too high, or right on the mark. Because they find out how accurate each guess is, census takers can move closer and closer to the real number of rice kernels on the table. Moving flocks of birds will not agree to sit still while people test the accuracy of their guesses. But the accuracy gained through "rice testing" has been found to improve census estimates made in the field.

When it comes to social intelligence, I think most of us are probably like the basketball player who never watches to see if foul shots go in, or like the bird census taker who never counts the real number of rice kernels. I think that all of us tend to make social intelligence interpretations, but most of us lack the crucial habit of testing our accuracy. This oversight may be due to the partly unconscious nature of the way that we detect nonverbal clues. However, any conscious effort to improve our social intelligence can succeed only if we complete the third step of the active interpretation method. In order to improve, we must attempt interpretations *and also* test the accuracy of these attempts.

This book was designed with this principle in mind. Each social intelligence question in this volume gives us a chance to guess the answer and also a chance to find out whether or not our guess is correct. In this way, the format of this book provides a model of the active interpretation method. I hope that the questions in this book will serve as a starting point for the many social intelligence opportunities of everyday life. I hope that this book will help you recognize these opportunities when they occur, so that you can continue to exercise, test, and improve your social intelligence.

There are many other fascinating areas of social intelligence, which for reasons of space could not be included in one book. To offer some examples, we have not examined the decoding and interpretation of emotions, various ways of reading the clues to a person's background and individuality, and the question of whether or not women are better than men at certain kinds of social intelligence. However, I am working on these and other social intelligence topics, and I plan to discuss them in a second volume.

SUGGESTED READING

Akeret, Robert U. *Photoanalysis*. New York: Simon & Schuster, Fireside Books, 1973.
How to read the psychological meaning of personal photographs like those found in a family album.

Archer, Dane, and Akert, Robin. "Words and Everything Else: Verbal and Nonverbal Cues in Social Interpretation." *Journal of Personality and Social Psychology* 35(1977): 443-49.
This article describes some of the research we have done using videotapes of people in various situations. In this study, we found experimental evidence that accurate interpretations require non-verbal clues—words alone are insufficient. This research is also described in the October 1977 issue of *Psychology Today*.

Ekman, Paul, and Friesen, Wallace V. *Unmasking the Face*. Englewood Cliffs, N.J.: Prentice-Hall, 1975.
A guide to the meaning of various facial expressions. Illustrated with photographs.

Goffman, Erving. *Gender Advertisements*. New York: Harper & Row, Publishers, 1978.
Goffman presents a fascinating analysis of advertising photographs (hundreds are reproduced), and he discovers consistent and often unexpected differences between the ways men and women are portrayed.

———. *Relations in Public*. New York: Harper & Row, Publishers, 1971.
Goffman analyzes the micro-sociology of daily life, focusing on the face-to-face rituals involved in "normal" behavior.

Henley, Nancy M. *Body Politics: Power, Sex, and Nonverbal Communication.* Englewood Cliffs, N.J.: Prentice-Hall, 1977.
A description of some important differences between the nonverbal behavior of men and women.

Knapp, Mark L. *Nonverbal Communication in Human Interaction.* New York: Holt, Rinehart & Winston, 1972.
An excellent summary of recent research on vocal clues, facial expressions, and other channels of nonverbal communication.

Rosenthal, Robert; Hall, Judith; DiMatteo, M. Robin; Rogers, Peter L.; and Archer, Dane. *Sensitivity to Nonverbal Communication: The PONS Test.* Baltimore: Johns Hopkins University Press, 1979.
This scientific book reports the result of a massive Harvard University research project on individual differences in the ability to decode nonverbal communication. This research is based on a film test (the Profile of Nonverbal Sensitivity or PONS) of the ability to recognize two-second glimpses of various emotions.